DISCARD

CULTURES OF THE WORLD

JAMAICA

Sean Sheehan

#33 4 MARSHALL CAVENDISH
New York • London • Sydney

Reference edition published 1994 by
Marshall Cavendish Corporation
2415 Jerusalem Avenue
P.O. Box 587
North Bellmore
New York 11710

© Times Editions Pte Ltd 1994

Originated and designed by
Times Books International, an imprint of
Times Editions Pte Ltd

Printed in Singapore

Library of Congress Cataloging-in-Publication Data:
Sheehan, Sean.
    Jamaica / Sean Sheehan.
        p. cm.—(Cultures Of The World)
    Includes bibliographical references and index.
    Summary: Explores the geography, history,
    government, economy, and culture of Jamaica.
    ISBN 1-85435-581-3 — ISBN 1-85435-578-3 (set)
    1. Jamaica—Juvenile literature [1. Jamaica.]
I. Title. II. Series.
F1868.2.S47 1993
972.92—dc20   93–11019
                    CIP
                    AC

Cultures of the World

Editorial Director	Shirley Hew
Managing Editor	Shova Loh
Editors	Michael Spilling
	Winnifred Wong
	Falak Kagda
	Roslind Varghese
	Jenny Goh
	Sue Sismondo
Picture Editor	Yee May Kaung
Production	Edmund Lam
Design	Tuck Loong
	Ronn Yeo
	Felicia Wong
	Loo Chuan Ming
Illustrators	Jimmy Kang
	Andrew Leong
	Anuar bin Abdul Rahim
MCC Editorial Director	Evelyn M. Fazio

INTRODUCTION

Jamaica has emerged from centuries of colonial rule, first by the Spanish and then by the British, as the most culturally dynamic of all Caribbean societies. Over 80% of Jamaicans are black descendants of African slaves who were brought across the Atlantic to work on sugar plantations. After the abolition of slavery, Indian and Chinese laborers were brought in, contributing to the remarkable array of faces in Jamaica.

The spirit of its people has expressed itself in a variety of cultural forms, of which reggae music and Rastafarianism are the most renowned. Looking beyond dance and music, the Jamaicans are a complex and serious people with a rich cultural tradition that continues to be celebrated. This book in the *Cultures of the World* series is part of that celebration. It looks at the island's unhappy past, its economy and government, its unique language, and the fascinating and exuberant ways in which ordinary Jamaicans live.

CONTENTS

Jamaica's wide variety of fruits and vegetables adds to its rich food heritage.

CONTENTS

Colorful wooden fish models at the craft market in Ocho Rios.

GEOGRAPHY

SET IN THE CARIBBEAN SEA, the island of Jamaica is 146 miles long from east to west and 50 miles wide from north to south at its widest. It forms part of the arc of islands that stretches from Cuba to Trinidad and Tobago.

Jamaica and the other islands in the West Indies owe their existence to earthquakes and volcanic activity. The potential for further quakes is still very real. Kingston, the capital of Jamaica, was destroyed by an earthquake in 1907.

ONCE UPON A TIME

Approximately 70 million years ago, a cataclysmic upheaval deep in the earth produced the mountain range that now forms the backbone of Mexico and Central America. One branch of this range extended eastward to what is now Jamaica. Most of it was submerged under water, but the higher peaks, such as those in the Blue Mountains in eastern Jamaica, remained above sea level.

The volcanic activity also caused the folding of terrain in some places and raised the seabeds. The elevated seabeds became a vast cemetery of marine life forms. Over millions of years, the skeletons of minute organisms formed a layer of white limestone. This limestone cap was pushed up from the sea by further movements of the earth about 20 million years ago.

The topography of Jamaica is the result of these very ancient events. About half of the island's land rises 1,000 feet above sea level.

THREE REGIONS

There are three main geographical regions in Jamaica: the Eastern Highlands, the Central Plateaus and Hills, and the Coastal Plains and Interior Valleys.

*We mus' tell map
We don't like we
position,
Please kindly take
we out o' sea
And draw we in
de Ocean.*

—Louise Bennett
*describing how
Jamaica is seen by
Jamaicans in a poem*

Opposite: **The crest of the Blue Mountain range acts as the main watershed in the eastern side of the island. Blue Mountain Coffee, one of the best in the world, is grown here.**

7

Above: **Aerial view of Cockpit Country, which consists of 500 square miles of land within the parishes of Trelawney, St. Elizabeth, and St. James.**

Opposite: **Bamboo rafts were once used to bring bananas and other produce from the interior to the towns and ports. Today they are used to take tourists up river to enjoy the beauty of lush rainforest.**

EASTERN HIGHLANDS The Eastern Highlands, which cover about 20% of Jamaica, including St. Thomas, St. Andrew, and Portland, rise to over 5,000 feet. The region is dominated by the Blue Mountain Ridge, the highest point of which is the Blue Mountain peak standing at 7,400 feet. To the far east of the Eastern Highlands are the John Crow Mountains. Running to the southeast is the Port Royal mountain range, which provides a scenic background to Jamaica's capital, Kingston. The vegetation and steepness of the mountains make them almost impenetrable. Departing from the beaten path is hazardous. One Jamaican novelist says, "If you move a yard off the paths you need a machete, and trying to cut your way through the tangle of fairy bamboo makes as much sense as running into a barbed wire fence...."

The mountains dissect Jamaica along an east-west axis, forming a watershed for more than 120 rivers. The rivers descend so steeply from the mountains that few are navigable. They cut their way through the northern or southern coastal plains into the Caribbean Sea. Two of the more well-known rivers are the Rio Grande and the Yallahs River.

KARST SCENERY IN THE CENTRAL PLATEAUS Limestone, which makes up most of the island of Jamaica, can be easily eroded by rain, as rain contains weak acids. The resulting landscape takes on a characteristic form that is known as karst scenery, named after a district in the former Yugoslavia where the limestone erosion process was studied in detail.

The limestone plateau in west Jamaica's Cockpit Country is dominated by numerous small rounded hills and larger hollows (cockpits). The deep hollows and rocky outcrops of land have combined to make the area unsuitable for habitation or agriculture.

Karst landforms occur because of the way rainwater works its way down and through the cracks in the limestone. Over a period of time, cracks develop into tunnels and caves. Rivers follow these underground passages and re-emerge where the rock is impermeable. Eventually, large areas of limestone are worn away, exposing the underlying rock. The paths of rivers in karst country are particularly fascinating. Take, for example, Hector's River. It starts in the central plateau, runs westward for 12 miles before disappearing into a sinkhole, then reappears in the south as One Eye River. It sinks again to travel underground one more mile, then reappears in the west to form the headwaters of the Black River.

Although the karst area of Jamaica does not encourage settlement, its inhospitabilness made it a good hiding place for the Maroons, the freed or runaways slaves, escaping from slavery in the 17th and 18th centuries.

THE COASTAL PLAINS AND INTERIOR VALLEYS The plains are narrow in the north and broader in the south. The most extensive lowland region stretches westward from Liguanea Plain near Kingston to about the midpoint of southern Jamaica. The most important farming region is in the western Black River Valley of St. Elizabeth and the Savanna-la-Mar area of Westmorland.

The river basins of the central plateaus also provide valuable agricultural land in the interior valleys and plains. They include the Queen of Spains Valley in the northwest, Nassau Valley to the south of Cockpit Country, and St. Thomas-in-the-Vale in eastern Jamaica.

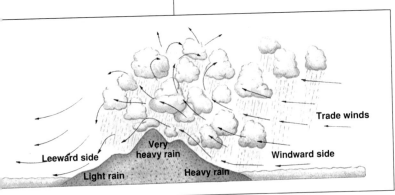

Above: **Trade winds bring rainfall to the Blue Mountains: heavy on the windward side, and light on the leeward side.**

Opposite: **High winds and waves are common during the hurricane season, from June to November.**

CLIMATE

As on other Caribbean islands, temperatures in Jamaica range from 75°F to 85°F during the day and drop to around 65°F at night, rarely falling below 60°F. Temperatures do not vary significantly during the year. Altitude affects the temperature—the general rule being that every ascent of 300 feet brings a reduction of 1°F. This partly explains why the more exclusive suburbs of Kingston, Jamaica's capital, are found in the surrounding foothills where daytime temperatures are cooler. The highest points on the island, the summits of the Blue Mountains, occasionally have light frost in the winter months.

Due to the continually warm climate, Jamaicans do not have to change to warmer clothing during the winter months. Nevertheless, they have to be prepared for heavy and sudden rainfall. The influence of the trade winds and topography is significant and needs to be understood.

TRADE WINDS Trade winds blow from the northeast towards the equator where they are deflected westward by the rotation of the earth. When they reach the Blue Mountains, they are forced to rise. As the air mass ascends, it cools considerably and the moisture in the air condenses and falls as rain. Most of the rain falls on the windward side of the mountain range. By the time the air mass reaches the other side, little moisture is left. The leeward area remains relatively dry. This is why Port Antonio in the northeast receives about 130 inches of rain annually, while Kingston in the southeast receives about 30 inches. The mountains receive about 200 inches of rain.

HURRICANES Hurricanes threaten Jamaica from June to November. They usually hit the eastern end of the island first and then move northward before dying out. The arrival of a hurricane is heralded by a sultry atmosphere, with a darkening sky and low clouds as the storm approaches. The rain and high winds of the hurricane are broken momentarily as the calm storm center passes overhead. Once the eye of the storm has passed, the fierce winds return until the storm travels on and the wind gradually dies down.

A hurricane develops when a strong upward air current creates a space into which new air is drawn. If this happens further than eight degrees from the equator, the new air is deflected by the force of the earth's rotation and it turns inward, spiralling in a counter-clockwise direction. The wind speed can quickly reach 75 miles an hour, and 200 miles an hour near the center. The storm can cover an area of 50 to 500 miles and last for days. Although the winds reach terrific speeds, the storm itself moves relatively slowly, perhaps only 10 miles a day. When hurricanes move very slowly over land, the worst damage is inflicted on people and property.

Hurricane Gilbert, one of the most ferocious storm ever recorded in the Western Hemisphere, hit Jamaica in September 1988. Over 30 people were killed, 100,000 homes were destroyed and about 20% of the island's population became homeless.

FLORA AND FAUNA

Woodland forest once covered most of the island but little of it now remains. In the southern coastal regions, however, mangrove trees continue to flourish because there is no economic incentive to cut them down. Normally plants cannot survive in seawater, but mangroves are able to live along the muddy coastline and cope with the salt in a variety of ways. Some types of mangroves have "filters" that protect their root system, while other species take in the salt only to excrete it through their leaves or expel it by dropping the leaves that are saturated with salt.

In the west and southwest, where the land is not suitable for agriculture, there are level areas of grassland scattered with isolated scrub trees. This is known as savanna country.

A more attractive feature of Jamaican flora is the ceiba or silk cotton tree that often grows to a huge size. Circumferences of 50 feet and heights of 130 feet are common. There is even a road in Kingston called Half Way Tree Road that recalls the days when a huge ceiba tree was the resting place for women traveling into the capital with their market produce. Ceiba seeds are surrounded by a very light, fluffy material that is used to fill life jackets and cushions. The tree is not planted for commercial exploitation in Jamaica.

Jamaica has more than 3,000 species of flowering plants, including 200 varieties of orchids and over 450 species of ferns. The national flower of Jamaica is the *lignum vitae*, meaning "the wood of life." It has purple blossoms and bright yellow stamens. In the past, the plant was highly valued for its medicinal properties.

Thick mangrove swamp on the Black River in the parish of St. Elizabeth. Mangrove plants have evolved ways of living in a saltwater environment.

Plants that are cultivated for their commercial and domestic value include coffee, banana, cocoa, yam, okra, and ginger. Other noticeable plants and trees are the breadfruit tree, mango, pawpaw, and guava. Common fruits are the orange, grape, melon, and starfruit. Most of these plants are not native to Jamaica but were introduced into the island.

Similarly, many of Jamaica's animals are not indigenous, and those that are native to the island, such as the manatee and the crocodile, are becoming increasingly rare. Far more common nowadays is the mongoose, a ferret-like carnivore brought to the island from India to kill rats and snakes that infested the cane fields.

There are over a thousand species of fireflies around the world and Jamaica's fauna includes 14 different varieties. Each species has its own lighting system characterized by a particular color, intensity and interval between flashes.

BIRDS AND JAMES BOND

The birds on the island are divided into two groups: migratory and indigenous.

There are two migratory periods in the year. In autumn, birds from North America fly south to the grasslands of Brazil and the marshes of La Plata, Argentina. Their flight route is nearly 7,000 miles long and does not follow the continental land mass. Upon reaching Florida and the other Gulf States, the birds fly across the Gulf of Mexico, passing over Cuba and Jamaica. About one third of the 60 different species of birds that follow this migratory route stay in Jamaica for the winter. In spring, these birds return to the north using the same flight route.

One of the 25 indigenous species is Jamaica's national bird, the streamer-tailed hummingbird. It is more commonly known as the Doctor Bird, perhaps because of its black head, recalling the days when doctors wore black top hats, and its divided tail that resembles a stethoscope. The bird is featured on the Jamaican dollar bill and the Air Jamaica logo.

Another bird that has its own Jamaican nickname is a crow known as the John Crow. It has a black plumage tinged with brown, while its feet, naked head, and neck are purplish red. It looks a little like a turkey. John Crows are scavengers and often can be seen rummaging in garbage dumps. The rarely seen albino John Crow is called John Crow Headman, which is a dig at the white colonialists of Jamaica.

Ian Fleming, the writer who created the character of secret agent James Bond, lived in Jamaica for many years. He wrote all his Bond novels on the island and named his hero James Bond after the author of one of his favorite books, *Birds of the West Indies*. The Bond movie, *Live and Let Die*, was filmed in Jamaica.

LIFE IN THE WATER

The Caribbean Sea that surrounds Jamaica is extremely clear, and sunlight can penetrate to a depth of 80 feet. Floating on the surface, yellow clumps of drifting seaweed called sargassum are very common. Fishes often swim along with the sargassum seeking out the multitude of tinier fishes and shrimps that inhabit the seaweed.

Sargassum is harmless. Not so the Portuguese man-of-war (*Physalia physalis*) that can be found in the waters around Jamaica. It resembles a large jellyfish but is actually a colony of organisms, each with a specialized function. One part of it secretes gas into an organ known as the "float" that allows the colony to drift on the surface of the water with the current. Other members of the colony produce tentacles that trail along under the water and kill fish on contact. Anyone accidentally touching the tentacles receives an especially nasty and painful sting.

A different marine animal that is actively sought out by snorkelers is

coral. This tiny animal's supporting skeleton is formed out of the limestone in seawater, and it often joins up with other corals to form a co-ordinated structure. Corals that live on reefs have microscopic plant cells living on them, and they share the nutrients made by aquatic plants. Some corals in the Caribbean float freely, displaying their lovely colors.

Tropical fish and lobsters inhabit the numerous crevices in the reef and attract sharks and barracudas. Parrotfish break off tiny pieces of the reef and swallow it in order to digest the tiny plant life that clings to the rock. At night, the fish wraps itself in a mucous cocoon that protects it against predators.

The Port Royal mountain range provides a scenic backdrop for Kingston, the capital of Jamaica.

JAMAICAN TOWNS

Urban life in Jamaica is concentrated along the coastal regions where the fertile and more level land allows for commercial development of crops. Recent decades have seen the development of tourist towns. Montego Bay, Ocho Rios, and Port Antonio are all situated along the northern coast where the large sandy beaches have encouraged their growth as tourist centers. Jamaica's main roads follow the coastline, except in the south where they run farther inland. Only two major roads run in a north-south direction, connecting the central towns.

KINGSTON The seat of government moved from Spanish Town (*Villa de la Vega*) to Kingston in 1872, and since then Kingston has been the capital of Jamaica. It lies in the southeastern corner of the island and is the largest English-speaking center south of Miami. Its area of over 10 square miles acts as the nucleus of commercial and cultural life on the island. Kingston grew out of the ashes of disaster. In 1907, the city was rebuilt after suffering

an earthquake, several fires and hurricanes. Today, it is a picturesque town with the Port Royal mountain range in the background and the seventh largest natural harbor in the world as its waterfront.

The University of West Indies, founded in 1948, is located in Kingston. The campus occupies a square mile of land that once belonged to the Hope sugar estate. An aqueduct constructed in the 17th century to carry water to the Hope estate is still present in the university grounds.

PORT ANTONIO Situated on the northeastern coast, Port Antonio overlooks twin harbors (West and East Harbor). Navy Island, situated in West Harbor, once belonged to Hollywood actor Errol Flynn.

Port Antonio was a busy and thriving port at the peak of the banana trade in the early part of the 20th century. However, several hurricanes in the 1930s and an imported banana disease known as the Panama Disease contributed to the decline of the banana trade. Today, like most towns on the northern coast, the main industry of Port Antonio is tourism.

Picturesque Port Antonio and its twin harbors. On the lower right of the picture is Navy Island.

MONTEGO BAY Jamaica's second largest town is also its foremost tourist resort and ranks as one of the most well-known holiday destinations in the Caribbean. It is characterized by a string of luxury beach hotels, designer boutiques, and private homes in closely guarded compounds. The contrast between the lifestyle in Montego Bay and that in the slums that fringe most other towns in Jamaica is very dramatic.

Columbus called the bay "El Golfo de Bueno Tiempo," or good-weather gulf. The name Montego Bay may come from the word *manteca* (fat or lard), a by-product of the numerous wild hogs that roamed the region. Or it could be derived from the name of an early colonizer, Montego de Salamanca. The origin of the name has been lost over time.

The town has several historic sites, including the parish church, the Square Parade, and the Court House. Rose Hall, said to be haunted by the *duppy* (ghost) of its infamous owner Anne Palmer, is just 10 miles from Montego Bay. Anne Palmer is said to have tortured and murdered slaves and executed lovers she no longer favored before she was murdered.

PORT ROYAL This historic town resting at the end of a seven-mile long narrow strip of land south of Kingston was Jamaica's first trading city. Until June 7, 1692, when an earthquake and later a tidal wave struck the site, Port Royal was described as "the fairest town of all English plantations...." This former pirates' lair and British naval base was cleared and filled in for an airforce base, and the strip of land is now Jamaica's international airport. Port Royal is the site of large-scale restoration to make it an important historical attraction; this includes archeological work on land and underwater explorations for sunken treasure.

OCHO RIOS Ocho Rios (meaning "eight rivers") is erroneously believed to derive its name from the Spanish after they discovered eight rivers around the town. Actually, the Spanish gave it another name, Las Chorreras, or "the waterfalls," a reference to the Dunn's River Falls west of the town. This is a scenic and popular swimming spot for Jamaicans and tourists. One of Jamaica's biggest bauxite mines is located near Ocho Rios.

Above: **The Dunn's River Falls near Ocho Rios is a popular swimming and scenic spot.**

Opposite: **The white sandy beaches of Montego Bay make it a popular resort.**

DIEU SUR TOUT

Here Lyes the Body of LEWIS GALDY Esq.
who departed this Life at Port Royal
the 22. December 1739 Aged 80. He was Born
at Montpelier in France but left that
Country for his Religion & came to settle in
this Island where He was swallowed up in the
Great Earth-quake in the Year 1692 & By the
Providence of God was by another Shock
thrown into the Sea & Miraculously saved
by swimming until a Boat took him up; He
Lived many Years after in great Reputation
Beloved by all that knew him and much
Lamented at his Death.

HISTORY

LIKE THE TIP OF AN ICEBERG, only a small part of Jamaica's history is visible. On May 5, 1494, Christopher Columbus and his conquistadors arrived on the island, and the subsequent events have been well recorded. The island was a Spanish colony for 150 years, after which it was acquired by the British in 1655. It remained under British rule until 1962, when Jamaica became independent.

What lies buried in the mists of time is a record of the previous seven or eight centuries when Jamaica was home to the Arawaks.

Opposite: The tombstone of a Lewis Galdy records the huge earthquake of 1692 that swallowed Port Royal. It was believed that the violent end of the town was retribution for the wickedness of its residents.

Below: **A 1778 map of Jamaica.**

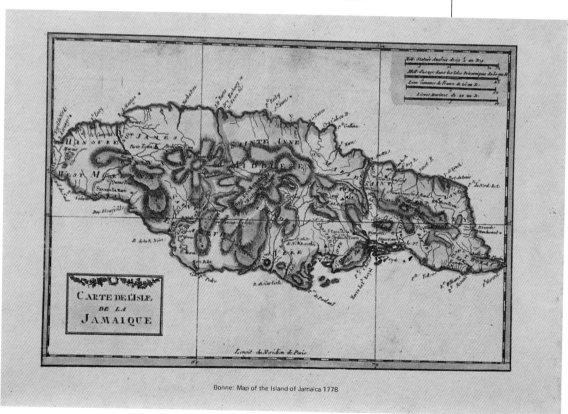

Bonne: Map of the Island of Jamaica 1778

THE ARAWAKS

The earliest known inhabitants of Jamaica were the Arawaks. Driven from their homelands in what is now Venezuela and the Guianas by other hostile Indian tribes, the Arawaks migrated north around 600 B.C. to 700 B.C. and eventually settled in Jamaica and the other Caribbean islands. The Arawaks, viewed as Indians by the Spanish invaders who thought they had sailed around the world to India, were a seagoing people who lived close to the coasts and rivers.

Arawak paintings that have survived on the walls of caves and other archeological finds make it clear that the Arawaks were skilled in producing tools and implements for everyday use. One of their inventions—a hanging bed of cotton suspended by cords at each end—made a deep impression on the Spanish, who brought the hammock back to Europe.

Between 60,000 and 100,000 Arawaks were living in Jamaica when the Spanish arrived. They had their own power structure that worked through a system of chiefs and sub-chiefs, and their skill in sailing allowed them

to barter with neighboring islanders. Nevertheless, none of this prepared them to deal with the Europeans who imposed their laws and religious beliefs on the Arawaks.

The Spanish invaders enslaved the Arawaks, and within a relatively short time, the Arawak population dwindled to a tiny minority. Many of the Arawaks simply died through overwork. Probably many more took to their canoes and left their island in the hope of escaping from the Europeans. Another factor contributing to their decline and eventual demise was their lack of immunity to ailments and diseases that the Spanish brought with them. The common cold became a deadly virus and decimated the native population.

There are no Arawaks left in Jamaica. The only signs of their existence come to light when archeologists discover their village sites or burial grounds. What little is known about their culture in Jamaica comes from the observations recorded by the Spanish.

Above: **Arawak painting on a cave wall.**

Opposite: **A replica of an Arawak hut in the National Museum.**

THE SPANISH ARRIVAL

There, silhouetted against the evening sky, arose sheer and darkly green Xamayca. It is the fairest island ... mountainous and ... very large, bigger than Sicily, and all full of valleys and fields and plains.

—Record of the first European sighting of Jamaica on May 5, 1494.

The Spanish came in search of gold, and when that did not materialize, they found comfort in the amazing fertility of the land. For the next 10 years, an average of 80 Spanish ships a year arrived in the Caribbean. It was the beginning of European colonization in Jamaica.

By 1515, there were so few Arawaks left that the Spanish began importing African slaves to replace them. By that time, the search for gold in Jamaica had been abandoned, and the Spanish who settled there were making money by exporting cattle and their hides. By the beginning of the 17th century, the Spanish had built a church and a monastery on the island.

Compared to the fabulous riches that were discovered elsewhere, the island of Jamaica had little to offer. It was only regarded as a valuable supply base, and while some money could be made from agriculture, the real wealth that was crossing the Atlantic to Spain was gold taken from Mexico after the Aztec rebellion there had been crushed. It was this wealth that attracted the English and other European imperialists to the Caribbean.

CHRISTOPHER COLUMBUS

Christopher Columbus was born in 1451 in Genoa, Italy. His lifetime ambition was to search for a westward route to India and the Orient for trade in the valuable spices of Asia. He made four trips across the Atlantic and visited Jamaica on two of them.

Columbus did not visit Jamaica on his first trip across the Atlantic. He did, however, visit Cuba and heard stories of a gold-rich island called Xaymaca. On his second trip to the Caribbean, he made a point of exploring the island and establishing contact with its inhabitants. He was disappointed not to find the gold he expected.

Columbus' next trip to Jamaica was eight years later, in 1502, and it was to be his last voyage across the Atlantic Ocean. The experience of revisiting Jamaica proved to be unfulfilling. After spending a year exploring the coast of Central America, his worm-eaten wooden ships became waterlogged and unfit for further journeys. He sought refuge in Jamaica, where he was forced to spend a year waiting to be rescued. During that time he had to put down two rebellions by his own men, and when he finally departed there was no one was left to go on calling the island Santiago—the name he had christened it.

After returning to Spain in 1504, Columbus became very ill. He was also denied credit or recognition for his explorations. He died two years later, still thinking that he had successfully found an alternate route to India and the East.

Subsequently, the king and queen of Spain presented his family with the entire island of Jamaica as a gift. Given the unhappy year Columbus spent on the island, it is doubtful whether he would have been delighted.

In 1992, to mark the 400 years since Columbus first arrived in the West Indies, celebrations and protests were organized in the Caribbean. Columbus' immortality was guaranteed, but to many he is a symbol of the greed and imperialism that radically altered the history and culture of the people who lived on islands like Jamaica.

Fort Charles, named after King Charles II, is the oldest fortified site in Port Royal. It was used as a lookout point to watch out for French and Spanish pirate ships trying to enter the harbor.

THE ENGLISH TAKEOVER

In 1655, an English army of 7,000 landed in Jamaica and put Spanish rule to an end. It was not the first time the English had raided the island, but this time Jamaica had been weakened by a series of attacks by pirates and the fleets of other European nations that sought to challenge Spanish supremacy in the West Indies. *Villa de la Vega*, then the capital of Jamaica (Spanish Town today), was captured in less than two days. Spain made two attempts to recapture Jamaica, but both failed.

THE MAROONS Land was given to the English soldiers and settlers who became farmers. The new invaders turned into defenders of their land, fighting off guerrilla attacks by the Spanish and freed African slaves.

Before the Spanish fled from the English invaders, they released and armed many of their slaves, who in turn raided the English plantations periodically and assisted in numerous slave rebellions. These African-Jamaican guerrillas became known as Maroons, a term that may have derived from the Spanish word *cimarrón*, meaning "wild and untamed," or *marrano*, meaning "wild boar."

Descendants of these early rebels still live in Jamaica, and the Land of the Maroons is a geographical region of the island.

Near Montego Bay, there is also an area known as the Land of Look Behind. The explanation for this goes back to the early days of English occupation when the English found themselves the targets of frequent surprise attacks by the Maroons. So when they went out on patrol, they adopted the habit of riding two persons on one mule, seated back-to-back. This was the only way they felt safe!

HENRY MORGAN

The most famous buccaneer was Henry Morgan (c. 1635–1688), who based himself at Port Royal and helped to make Jamaica synonymous with piracy. He not only led raids on Spanish ships but also attacked their settlements in Central America. In 1670, he actually captured Panama. The glamorous image often associated with the buccaneers comes partly from reckless and often courageous deeds. At the same time, pirates like Henry Morgan were ruthless and violent men who murdered for a living.

Sᵀ HEN: MORGAN

NO PREY, NO PAY

During the 17th century, Jamaica's history was linked closely to the activities of pirates who sailed the Caribbean. Buccaneers was the name given to those pirates who preyed on Spanish ships taking gold and other treasures from Mexico and South America back to Spain.

The buccaneers—mostly British and French—made their headquarters at Port Royal in Jamaica, which developed and prospered as a direct result of their activities. The buccaneers' ships could be safely harbored, and the settlement developed around the spending power generated by the buccaneers' raids and captured booty. As enemies of Spain, the pirates were valued by the British. This is why the term "privateer" was used to describe some of the buccaneers; although their ships were privately owned, they were indirectly encouraged by the British to attack Spanish ships.

The British government supported their activities unofficially until a treaty with Spain recognized Britain's right to hold possessions in the West Indies. Henry Morgan was knighted and appointed lieutenant-governor of Jamaica in 1674.

Four years after Morgan's death, an earthquake destroyed most of Port Royal, including Morgan's burial ground. Legends of treasures that sank to the bottom of the sea have fuelled numerous diving expeditions to recover the booty of Morgan and his fellow buccaneers.

ROGUES' GALLERY

Henry Morgan was not the only pirate associated with Jamaica, although those who came after him never enjoyed the sort of official recognition that eventually made Morgan a knight with the title of Sir Henry Morgan.

Edward Teach, better known as Blackbeard, was probably the most fearsome pirate of them all. He started his career in Jamaica. According to legend, he was a large man who added to his daunting appearance by going into battle with lighted matches plaited into his black beard and long hair!

Nicholas Brown stepped so far outside the law that a reward of £500, a vast sum of money at the time, was offered for his capture in Jamaica. He was caught and killed by John Drudge in Cuba. To ensure that he collected the reward, Drudge cut off Brown's head and pickled it in a keg of rum until it reached Jamaica.

Captain Jack Rackham, also known as Calico Jack, earned his nickname because of his fondness for calico underwear. When he was finally captured and brought to Jamaica for trial in 1720, it was discovered that two of his crew were women who had disguised themselves as men. It was said that the female pirates, Ann Bonney and Mary Read, were as rough and ruthless as their male counterparts.

Rackham was executed, and his corpse was publicly suspended in an iron frame to serve as an example to others. The spot where this happened is still known today as Rackham's Cay.

SUGAR AND SLAVES

It was the Spanish who first introduced sugarcane to Jamaica. The British encouraged its development because of the profit that could be made by exporting sugar to Europe. Sugar production, however, required a large labor force, and there was a severe labor shortage in Jamaica. By the 18th century the Arawak population had completely disappeared, and most of the early African slaves had negotiated their own freedom in the Maroon treaty of 1739.

The solution was found in the slave trade. British ships traveled to the west coast of Africa to collect slaves and transport them to the West Indies. Jamaica became the main auction center where the slaves were either sold to owners of sugar plantations or re-exported to other colonies.

The large sugar estates where the slaves were destined to spend the remainder of their lives were like miniature towns. High on a hill was the planter's homestead, while down below the slaves labored in the fields. The slaves had their own housing and small plots of land where they grew their own food.

In 1760, the slaves revolted under the leadership of Tacky, who had been a chief in Africa. Tacky was successful at first, but was later shot and killed. His band of men committed suicide rather than return to slavery.

The slave trade was finally abolished in 1807, but emancipation for Jamaica's slaves came only after another rebellion in 1838.

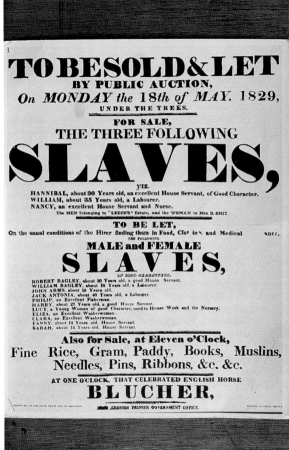

During the peak of the slave trade, Jamaica served as an auction center where slaves were bought by the local plantation owners or sold to other slave merchants.

Deputy Prime Minister Donald Sangster and Prime Minister Alexander Bustamante of Jamaica with U.S. President John F. Kennedy (1963).

TROUBLED TIMES

In the years after the abolition of slavery, it became apparent that social barriers set up against the African-Jamaicans were entrenched and difficult to remove. Freedom from slavery did not dramatically alter the lives of the thousands of African-Jamaicans who remained poor peasants.

Troubles mounted when both the government and missionaries tried to prevent the African-Jamaicans from observing their traditional Christmas celebrations in 1841. A riot broke out and many were wounded. Many African-Jamaicans began to see religion as a weapon of oppression and became hostile to the missionaries who had helped them attain freedom.

The ensuing years could be described as years of decay in Jamaica. Landowners (known as planters), who had always dominated Jamaica's House of Assembly, did their best to protect their own interests by resisting change. They worked the soil to exhaustion and paid their workers meager wages. There were rebellions by the workers in many parts of the island.

In 1865, another rebellion broke out in Morant Bay as the poverty-stricken masses demanded improvement in their way of life. The uprising was ruthlessly crushed, and hundreds were executed, including two of the leaders, Paul Bogle and George William Gordon, who are now national heroes. The House of Assembly was dissolved in 1866, and Jamaica became a Crown Colony.

When the Depression hit America and Europe in the 1930s, the price of sugar fell dramatically. This was one of the factors that added to the gloomy life experienced by most Jamaicans and led to further outbreaks of violence and racial tension.

Out of the turmoil emerged two individuals and two organizations that were to play crucial roles in the island's future. Alexander Bustamante organized the Bustamante Industrial Trade Union, which dock workers and laborers from the plantations quickly joined. Out of this movement, the Jamaican Labor Party was formed. The other major figure was Norman Manley, a lawyer, who founded the People's National Party. Both leaders pressed for social and political reforms. In 1944, a new Constitution came into being, and for the first time, every adult had the right to vote.

INDEPENDENCE

In 1958, Jamaica joined the West Indies Federation. Two years later, a referendum was held on Jamaica's continued membership in the Federation, which was beset with problems. Bustamante's Labor Party campaigned for a "No" vote, which was the outcome of the referendum.

A general election was held in April 1962, and the Jamaican Labor Party won not just the election but also the opportunity to head Jamaica's first independent government. On August 6, 1962, full independence was granted, and the Jamaican flag was flown. Two weeks of celebration followed as Jamaica became the 109th member of the United Nations.

"Independence wid a vengeance, Independence raisin' cain, Jamaica start grow beard, ah hope, We chin can sta' de strain."

—Louise Bennett expressing the proud mood felt by all Jamaicans on Independence Day in 1962.

GOVERNMENT

JAMAICA HAS BEEN INDEPENDENT since 1962 and is a member of the British Commonwealth. The Commonwealth is a voluntary association of countries that were once subject states of the British Empire. The countries maintain friendly links with the United Kingdom but remain independent. Jamaica has a governor-general who represents the Queen of England, but the position is purely ceremonial because it has no real executive powers. The appointment of governor-general is recommended by the prime minister of Jamaica.

Jamaica is a democracy, and a very vibrant one. Political discussions are animated and often dominated by the Jamaican Labor Party (JLP) and the People's National Party (PNP). Although their differences have led to outbreaks of violence at elections, the democratic ground rules are steadfastly observed. The country has a strong and healthy trade union movement, from which the two political parties were founded.

Opposite: **Located on Kingston's Duke Street, Jamaica's Parliament House, also known as Gordon House, was named in honor of rebel leader George William Gordon.**

Below: **Inside Parliament House.**

PARLIAMENTARY DEMOCRACY

The Jamaican Parliament is a bicameral one; that is, there are two legislative assemblies: a House of Representatives and a Senate. The 60-member House is elected by adult suffrage—citizens over the age of 18 have the right to vote for their representatives in Parliament. The Senate has 21 seats. The political

ORGANIZATION OF THE JAMAICAN GOVERNMENT

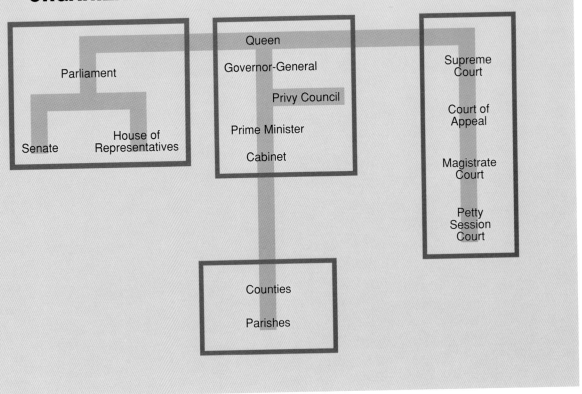

Parliament

Senate   House of Representatives

Queen

Governor-General

Privy Council

Prime Minister

Cabinet

Supreme Court

Court of Appeal

Magistrate Court

Petty Session Court

Counties

Parishes

party that wins the most votes in the general election is able to appoint 13 members of the Senate to ensure it has a majority representation.

The bicameral Parliament is a legacy of Jamaica's colonial past as it is based on the British Parliament. The House of Representatives, led by the Prime Minister, is the elected government and the main legislative body of the country. The Senate, unlike the United States Senate, has no real democratic power in that its members are appointed, not elected, and its decisions can be overruled by the House of Representatives. The main role of the Senate is to debate and sanction legislation proposed by the House of Representatives.

Local government is also subject to the democratic process. Three administrative areas called counties—Cornwall in the west, Middlesex in the center, and Surrey in the east—are divided into 13 parishes and the incorporated areas of Kingston and St. Andrew. Elected councils administer the local government with grants from the central government for essential services such as water, health, sanitation, and fire protection.

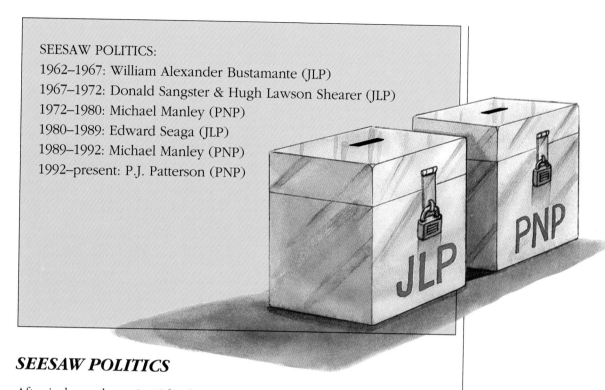

SEESAW POLITICS:
1962–1967: William Alexander Bustamante (JLP)
1967–1972: Donald Sangster & Hugh Lawson Shearer (JLP)
1972–1980: Michael Manley (PNP)
1980–1989: Edward Seaga (JLP)
1989–1992: Michael Manley (PNP)
1992–present: P.J. Patterson (PNP)

SEESAW POLITICS

After independence in 1962, the JLP led by William Alexander Bustamante won power and retained it for nine years. Bustamante had a magnetic personality, and his ability to speak on the level of ordinary Jamaicans won him much popularity in the early years.

In 1972, the PNP swept to power, and Michael Manley became the prime minister. Manley, a charismatic leader and a socialist, initiated many economic and social reforms that set out to redress the imbalance between the rich and the poor in Jamaica. Minimum wages were established, and the rights of trade unionists were consolidated. Jamaica became an active member of the nonaligned movement, a group of governments opposed to the Cold War between the United States and the former Soviet Union.

Manley's sympathy towards Cuba and the Soviet Union, added to the PNP's socialist policies, upset many business interests. Valuable international and American aid began to diminish.

All these factors added up to cause economic hardship for many Jamaicans. In the 1980 election, the JLP returned to power and reversed many of the PNP's policies.

The police, affectionally called the Red Stripes because of the red seams decorating the trousers of their blue uniform, have a record of loyal and honest service, despite the rising tide of crime and violence in the cities.

The change in policies was most apparent in the field of foreign affairs. The leader of the JLP, Edward Seaga, was the first head of state to visit the then newly elected President of the United States, Ronald Reagan in 1980. When Reagan later repaid the courtesy by visiting Jamaica, he became the first American president to ever officially visit the island. The pro-American stance of the JLP was also signalled by the closing of the Cuban Embassy in Jamaica.

By 1989, it was evident to Jamaicans that the JLP was no more successful at managing the economy than the party they had displaced in 1980. In addition, the devastation caused by Hurricane Gilbert in 1988 resulted in a significant drop in Jamaica's export earnings from agriculture, mining, and the service sector. Government spending on health and schools had been sharply reduced, and other adverse economic conditions prevented the JLP from returning to power in the 1989 election.

The present prime minister of Jamaica is Percival James Patterson. He was sworn in on March 30, 1992 as the country's first black prime minister and won a landslide victory in the general elections in 1993.

THE MANLEYS

The People's National Party was founded by Norman Washington Manley in 1938. The party led the nationalist campaign for independence from Britain, and it was Norman Manley (right), a lawyer, who drafted a revised Constitution that prepared the way for independence in 1962. Nevertheless, the first election saw the victory of the rival Jamaican Labor Party led by Alexander Bustamante. Norman Manley died before his own party won power in 1972.

Bustamante was Norman Manley's cousin; in fact three of Jamaica's first five prime ministers—Alexander Bustamante, Michael Manley, and Hugh Shearer—were from the same family. Both Norman Manley and Alexander Bustamante are considered the fathers of modern Jamaica.

Norman Manley's son, Michael, became prime minister in 1972. He was a flamboyant politician whose rhetoric held audiences spellbound. He was given the biblical nickname Joshua and hailed as the prophet-politician who would lead his country to salvation. His socialist policies, however, conflicted with those of the International Monetary Fund (IMF) and the Western allies. When the necessary loans could not be secured, Jamaica came close to bankruptcy. By the time he lost power in 1980, unemployment had risen to over 30%. Manley accused the United States Government of secretly destabilizing Jamaica because of his sympathy toward Cuba and the Soviet Union.

After his defeat in 1980, Manley led a very determined opposition to the rule of the JLP. He continued to champion the rights of the poor, and his party's slogan for the 1989 election, "We put PEOPLE first," was in marked contrast to the JLP's slogan, "You need cash to care."

The difference between Michael Manley's first government (1972–1980) and his second one (1989–1992) was very significant. In his second term of office, he worked amiably with the IMF and accepted the case for a free market economy and curbs on government spending. Unfortunately, his health declined and it came as no surprise when he passed the mantle of power to his deputy prime minister, P.J. Patterson, in 1992. The era of Manley politics, which had lasted for over 50 years, finally came to an end.

Graffiti on walls is a common way of expressing dissatisfaction with government policies.

POLITICAL PASSIONS AND GANGSTERS

Like many Latin Americans, Jamaicans are passionate about their country's politics. Unfortunately, Jamaican politics has acquired a notorious reputation for bringing violence onto the streets. This reputation was largely created out of the events surrounding the elections of 1976 and 1980, when rival gangs belonging to the two parties conducted their campaigns not only with speeches and statements but also with guns.

The violence that accompanied these elections scared not only the vast majority of Jamaicans but also the tourists. As the scenes of fighting and killing were broadcast around the world, people who were considering a vacation in Jamaica were naturally deterred. Tourism, a mainstay of the economy, was badly affected, but it has since recovered.

During the 1976 election period, a gang of political zealots machine-gunned the house where Bob Marley, the country's international reggae star, was staying. Marley survived the attack and later wrote about the assassination attempt in a song entitled *Ambush in the Night.*

38

During the 1980 election campaign, Bob Marley again confronted the political gangsters by calling for peace. He held a concert at which he summoned the leaders of the two parties to the stage to join in singing *One Love.*

Despite the peace efforts, the 1980 election was marred by even more violence than the previous one.

HUMAN RIGHTS

The violence and turmoil that have characterized Jamaican politics understandably led many people to think the country has a weak democratic base. In fact, the opposite is true. Jamaica has an excellent record of human rights, and there is widespread respect for civil rights.

The Jamaican legal system, like its government, is modelled on the British system. Justice is administered by a system of courts, ranging from small local courts to a court of appeal and a Supreme Court, which is the final court of appeal. The judiciary is a separate branch of the government to ensure that the courts are free of political influence and that civil rights are upheld.

One exception occurred during the 1980 election when a state of emergency was declared in an attempt to curb political violence. A special Gun Court was set up with powers that curtailed some basic human rights. These special powers were aimed at controlling the political gangsters who threatened to undermine the democratic system.

Since the 1970s and 1980s, the degree of political violence has lessened considerably. At all elections, the secret ballot is rigidly adhered to and there is never any doubt that the counting of votes has been carried out fairly and legally.

The Jamaican Constitution guarantees the rights of the individual with regard to free speech and movement. The individual is guaranteed the right not to be imprisoned without a fair trial.

ECONOMY

ALTHOUGH JAMAICA'S ECONOMY traditionally has been dependent on agriculture, namely on sugar production, mining and tourism are now the main contributors to the island's income. Industrial products such as chemicals, fertilizers, and tires also earn Jamaica valuable foreign currency.

About 20% of Jamaica's workforce is still employed in agriculture. Besides sugarcane, Jamaica's cash crops are bananas, cacao, citrus fruits, coconuts, coffee, and yams. Jamaican rum, a by-product of sugar, is well-known and sold throughout the world.

MINING

The mining of bauxite is Jamaica's main industry and a crucial source of income. From bauxite, a mineral compound called alumina is extracted and used to produce aluminum, a versatile and important metal. Aluminum is lightweight, easily worked, and resistant to corrosion. It is used for a wide variety of products, ranging from the foil used to wrap foods to aircraft and automobiles.

In Jamaica, deposits of bauxite are generally found near the surface and mined by the open-cast method in which the topsoil and covering sand or clay are removed, and mechanical shovels are used to scoop out the ore. Unfortunately, large gashes are left behind in the land, exposing it to erosion.

After excavation, the next stage is the separation process, where the mined ore is mixed with caustic soda and heated until a solution of alumina is obtained. This solution contains a considerable amount of impurities that are removed by filtration. The remaining alumina solution undergoes precipitation to separate alumina from the solution, then calcination to burn off moisture. Alumina finally emerges as a white powder.

Jamaica is the world's second largest producer of bauxite. Bauxite companies are required by law to rehabilitate mined-out land, and they invest large sums of money to restore land to pasture, crop land, or forest.

Opposite: **Jamaica has one of the richest deposits of bauxite in the world. The open-cast method of mining is possible as the deposits occur near the surface.**

41

When bauxite was first mined in Jamaica in 1953, over one million tons of alumina were obtained. The figure rose to 16 million tons in 1976 but dropped to 6 million tons in 1986 because political tensions in the country closed many of the mines.

The process of turning alumina into aluminum requires huge amounts of electric power. Since most of Jamaica's power is generated from imported fuels, it is very expensive to produce electricity. Consequently, most of the alumina is exported to the United States and other industrialized countries where it is processed into aluminum and sold.

Another mineral mined in Jamaica is gypsum, found either as crystals or as a fine-grained substance called alabaster. The translucent character and soft texture of alabaster allows it to be sculpted and polished by hand for decorative purposes. When partly dehydrated, gypsum forms plaster of paris, a quicksetting plaster used in casts and to make reproductions.

TOURISM—BLESSING OR BLIGHT?

Jamaica's congenial climate attracts visitors throughout the year, and resorts like Montego Bay are internationally renowned. Tourism employs many Jamaicans and accounts for a considerable portion of the country's income.

It is debatable, however, just how beneficial tourism is to island nations like Jamaica. Most of the hotels are owned by foreign companies that, more often than not, repatriate profits. Thus, little money is set aside for local developments.

Windsurfing boats on the beach at Wyndam Rose Hall Hotel, Montego Bay.

While tourism provides a much needed source of employment, workers' income levels are very low. The comparative wealth of tourists, particularly those from the United States, serves to highlight the poverty of most islanders. Jamaicans working in the tourist areas are constantly exposed to a lifestyle that appears glamorous and admirable. The contrast in lifestyles can be a source of resentment and even a reminder of the black servitude suffered in the past.

Despite its disadvantages, tourism remains a vital part of Jamaica's economy because it enables Jamaica to diversify from agriculture. In 1981, the government reorganized the tourism agencies to provide better service for tourists. It also encouraged companies involved in tourism to consider the social and environmental effects of their activities.

SUGAR

Sugarcane and sugar beet plants produce a natural sugar called sucrose that is used extensively in food industries around the world. While sugar beets thrive best in a temperate climate, the tropical climate of Jamaica is ideal for the growth of sugarcane, a tall grass with a stout jointed stalk that stores sucrose.

Sugar was to the 17th and 18th centuries what oil is to the 20th century. The immense wealth generated from sugar production made the Caribbean Islands a valuable part of the British Empire.

The growth of the sugar industry also changed the racial composition and social structure in the producing countries. Ownership of the vast plantations was in the hands of a few rich colonists, while the canefields were worked by imported slaves.

In modern times, leading sugar-producing countries like the United States use machines to cut and harvest the sugar, but in Jamaica, people are still employed to cut the cane manually, often using a machete. It is very heavy yet poorly paid work.

Sugarcane harvesting with a machete is a back-breaking job.

Work conditions on the sugar estates are still very demanding. In 1990, a journalist who visited an estate about 30 miles west of Kingston reported that a 60-year-old cane cutter earned about $25 a week. After various deductions and tax, his take-home pay was half that amount. On a nearby plantation, a 54-year-old woman was left with just $1 from her previous week's earnings of $17.

SUGAR PRODUCTION

The first stage in the production of sugar, after the stalks have been cut and washed, involves shredding and crushing the stalks. This allows the juice to be extracted from the stalks. High-pressure water sprays help to dissolve the sugar from the stalks. The resulting cane juice, which is greatly diluted, is then ready for the next production stage.

To remove impurities, the juice is heated and lime is added. Later, the lime is removed by carbon dioxide. The diluted cane juice is filtered and sent to evaporation tanks where most of the water is removed, leaving a thick, syrupy juice. Heating removes the remaining water and allows the formation of sugar crystals.

The final stage involves placing the sugar crystals that formed in the syrup into a centrifuge. The high velocity spinning separates the crystals from the syrup, and the result, raw sugar, is almost pure sucrose. A further refining process involving additional diluting, filtering, evaporating, and spinning produces the pure white sugar we see in shops and supermarkets.

Molasses is the residual syrup left after raw sugar is obtained. It is used as stock feed, especially for dairy cows, or distilled for alcohol (rum). Bagasse, the dry cane fiber, is used for chipboard and fuel.

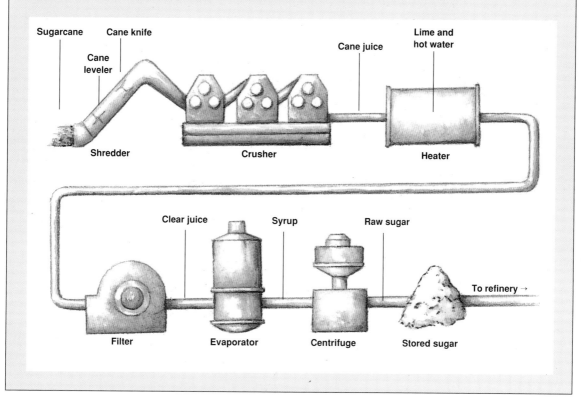

ECONOMIC PROBLEMS

The gross national product (GNP) per capita of a country is the money value of all the goods and services it produces in a given year divided by its population. Based on this measure, Jamaica is a poor country. The GNP per capita for Jamaica in 1988 was $1,080, while that of the United States, for example, was $19,840.

Jamaica also has a very unequal distribution of income, with the richest 5% of the population having 32% of the national income. The 1972–1980 government under Michael Manley attempted to alter the country's economy in favor of a more equitable distribution of wealth, but it met with little success. By 1980, the economy was in an even more perilous state, and critics allege that Jamaica only managed to survive because of illegal shipments of marijuana to the United States, which were worth at least $150 million a year.

The JLP government under the leadership of Edward Seaga adopted a very different approach to the island's economic ills. Control of the economy by the government was abandoned in favor of a free market. Free Zones were created and foreign firms were encouraged to set up factories. Over 30,000 jobs were created, especially in the clothing industry, and large numbers of women were employed.

Wages, however, were still extremely low. Women in a garment factory earned, on average, just over $10 a week after deductions, and yet a shirt for a child cost half that amount and a pair of shoes even more. Sweaters made by them were sold in the United States for $50, and "designer" sweaters assembled in the Free Zone were sold in America for $200.

It soon became clear that the new policies brought little, if any, positive change for the economically-disadvantaged Jamaicans.

THE ECONOMIC FUTURE

The new government that took over in 1989 has been more successful in managing Jamaica's economy. The budget deficit has been considerably reduced, and the economy is expected to maintain a growth rate of 2%. However, the rate of inflation has increased dramatically without a corresponding wage increase, so the standard of living for Jamaicans has actually declined.

The growth areas in the Jamaican economy are the tourist and bauxite industries. Now that the country is politically more stable and violence has decreased, there is a tourist boom. At the same time, the world market price for bauxite has increased, and investment in the mining industry should bring future dividends. For the average citizen, however, life continues to be hard. Many Jamaicans still see emigration to the United States and other countries as the answer to their problems.

Launch boats in the Bay of Grand Lido Hotel, Negril, provide short cruises for tourists along the southwest coast of Jamaica.

JAMAICANS

THE OVERWHELMING MAJORITY OF JAMAICANS are of African descent, but there is more of an ethnic mix than most people think. About 18% of the population is classed as *mulatto*, which is defined as the progeny of European masters and African slaves.

Another factor that contributed to the mixed genetic pool is the abolition of slavery in 1838. Landlords and plantation owners who were worried about a shortage of cheap labor turned elsewhere for replacements. Indians and Chinese, as well as poor Europeans, were imported into the country to replace African laborers. In time, these people intermarried with African-Jamaicans. Presently, there are significant minorities of African-Chinese and African-Indian Jamaicans.

Opposite: **The blending of different races over centuries has resulted in beauty such as this.**

Left: **Jamaican boys. The majority of Jamaicans are of African descent.**

OUT OF MANY, ONE PEOPLE

The Jamaican coat of arms bears the national motto "Out of Many, One People," a translation from the Latin phrase *Indus Uterque Serviet Uni.* It describes the different ethnic groups and mixed ancestry of most Jamaicans today. Indeed, the effect of intermarriage between the different races has resulted in a set of subtle gradations in skin color.

In the past, skin color was the basis for discrimination. Jamaicans of a lighter complexion were more likely to receive preferential treatment. Some mulattoes were sent overseas by their European fathers for a private education and then returned to elite positions in Jamaican society. Others were rewarded with better jobs simply because of their lighter skins. In the 1950s, for example, African-Jamaican protesters campaigned outside city offices for the employment rights of African-Jamaican girls, as only light-skinned mulattoes were employed to actually deal with customers in some workplaces such as banks and retail stores. The color prejudice also operated in churches, with whites occupying the front pews, mulattoes close behind, and blacks taking up the last remaining seats behind them.

At times, such prejudice caused discord and violence, but contemporary Jamaica is managing its racial mix more successfully than ever before. The days are now past when African-Jamaican girls straightened their hair and applied creams to lighten their skin.

FROM SLAVES TO CITIZENS

It was a Spanish priest who, in 1515, first suggested to the Spanish government that Africans could replace the rapidly dwindling number of Arawak laborers on the lucrative sugar plantations in the Caribbean. The ancestors of the majority of today's Jamaicans were natives of coastal West Africa, stretching from Senegal to the Congo, who were seized by European traders or sold by their chiefs. Although the slave trade itself ended between 1814 and 1830, the actual practice of slavery in the Caribbean did not stop immediately. Jamaica, like the other British colonies, only abolished slavery in 1838, while the Spanish colonies abolished slavery in 1886.

Long after the abolition of slavery, economic and political power remained in the hands of non-African Jamaicans. Even after independence in 1962, all three of the island's major sources of wealth—bauxite, sugar, and tourism—were under the control or influence of international corporations whose management did not include African-Jamaicans. In short, many African-Jamaicans who wanted to better themselves faced many social obstacles and prejudice.

The Universal Negro Improvement Association (UNIA), founded by the Jamaican Marcus Mosiah Garvey in 1914, played a significant role in changing the social and economic policies in Jamaica. The movement stressed the need for African-Jamaicans to shrug off the legacy of the slave trade and reassert their own cultural identity and individuality. In the 1970s, the Jamaican government attempted to redress this imbalance and inaugurated changes in the economy. The most significant change was

Cane cutters: a scene from the past and in the present. A popular independence slogan, "Massa Day Done, Better Must Come," conveys the euphoria of Jamaicans freed from colonial servitude. Yet "Better" has not come for many.

giving the state a degree of control over the island's bauxite industry and a share of the total production.

Garvey's ideas were so influential that they were the spiritual force of the Rastafarian movement. He also influenced black leaders in other countries—such as Malcolm X in the United States and Kwame Nkrumah, the first prime minister of Ghana.

The awareness perpetuated by the African-Jamaican movements and their resulting changes had tremendous repercussions for the consciousness of African-Jamaicans. They continue to play an important role in the way contemporary Jamaicans view themselves.

MARCUS MOSIAH GARVEY (1887–1940)

Garvey was employed as a printer until he founded the Universal Negro Improvement Association (UNIA) in 1914. At the time, the title was a grandiose one for a small group that proclaimed blacks would never achieve justice as long as white people were in a majority. "Back to Africa" was the rallying call for the movement's belief that black people should return to their African homelands.

At first, Garvey's organization did not attract a large following in Jamaica. In 1916, he went to the United States to spread his ideas, and by the 1920s he had over 12 million followers worldwide. Contributions flowed in, and the money was used to help set up all-black businesses, part of Garvey's campaign for self-reliance and independence from an economic system dominated by whites.

In 1925, Garvey was convicted of fraud in connection with the sale of stock in one of the businesses he had established. He was deported from the United States in 1927. He returned to Jamaica and attempted to enter national politics. Later, he moved to London where he died in obscurity in 1940. Garvey's body was eventually returned to Jamaica for burial in a mausoleum. He is considered one of the country's national heroes.

A direct descendant of the slaves freed by the Spanish.

MAROONS

Although the original Maroons in Jamaica were slaves who were freed by the retreating Spanish colonists, the term *maroon* is a general word for runaway slaves.

When the English attacked the Spanish colony of Jamaica in the 17th century, the African slaves, numbering perhaps 1,500, were released and armed in a final attempt to fight the English. After the Spanish fled, the slaves remained behind and joined the Maroons who had earlier escaped to the mountains. In time, they were joined by others who escaped from the slave-worked plantations created by the English. For many years, the Maroons conducted a guerrilla campaign against the new masters.

Maroon communities developed wherever plantations of slave labor existed. The Maroons of Jamaica are particularly noteworthy because of their independent status since the 18th century. While in the past this meant they were free individuals in the midst of a slave community, today their independence is from government control: Maroons govern themselves.

The Maroons of the 18th century managed to survive in the Blue Mountains and in Cockpit Country where the rugged terrain provided protection. The harsh conditions kept their population low, but their determination never to surrender ensured that they remained a thorn in the side of the slave owners. Eventually, the government made a treaty with Cudjoe, the leader of the Maroons in Cockpit Country, in 1739. They were granted 1,500 acres of land and the right to self-rule. They were also given a license to hunt within three miles of the town boundaries and to sell their produce in the markets.

One reason for the survival of the Maroons, apart from their own strong sense of independence, was the isolation of Cockpit Country. In recent years, of course, modern roads and transportation have broken down this natural barrier, and modern influences have weakened their sense of separateness. Employment opportunities, for example, are more likely to occur outside of Cockpit Country.

Accompong, one of the main Maroon villages in Cockpit Country since the 18th century, is a pilgrimage site for Maroons from all over the island on Cudjoe Day (January 6). On this day, celebrations are held to commemorate the signing of the peace treaty with the English. Today, the Maroons are gradually being integrated into the economic and social mainstreams of Jamaican life, but their unique history and special character are being preserved.

No one really knows the total number of Maroons on the island: estimates vary between 4,000 and 5,000.

ETHNIC MINORITIES

After the emancipation of Jamaica's slaves in 1838, many plantation owners turned to cheap white labor as a substitute workforce for those blacks who wanted nothing more to do with plantation life. Laborers were brought in from Ireland, Scotland, and other European countries. In Ireland, for instance, ships called at different ports and recruited workers with attractive promises—such as "a sow pig and the milk of a cow for each

Jamaicans of different complexions—the result of successive generations of mixed unions.

family"—made to those who agreed to emigrate to Jamaica. Some recruited Scottish and English were employed in skilled departments on the sugar estates, but the majority, along with the Irish and some Portuguese, were used as field labor.

Certain place names in Jamaica—Saxony, Bohemia, and Berlin, for example—bear testimony to the arrival of Germans on the island, and family names like Wedermeyer and Eldermayer can still be found today. Almost all the Germans who settled in Jamaica crossed the Atlantic as a result of the efforts of William Lemonius, who negotiated with an English landlord, Lord Seaford, for a grant of farming land. The new immigrants were peasants from the Rhineland who continued being farmers, eventually intermarrying with the native population. Like the Scottish and Irish, they arrived shortly after the slaves were freed. The few families of German descent that are still to be found in Jamaica today do not speak any German.

The arrival of Indian laborers began around the same time as the arrival of poor Europeans. Many of Jamaica's Indians are Christians, but some are still Moslems and Hindus and continue to celebrate their own festivals. The

NATIONAL COSTUME

Jamaican dress is generally conservative and characterized to some extent by the use of bright colors. Hats are popular with men and women. Women can be seen wearing broad, white, floppy hats and formal dresses on Sundays. Their Afro hairstyle betrays an African influence.

The woollen knitted hat, or "tam," is worn by many men, in particular by Rastafarians. The most spectacular feature of Rastafarian male dress, however, is the hairstyle. The hair is washed with soap that is allowed to dry in the hair before being tied into tight knots or braids. These "dreadlocks," as they are called, were copied from the Masai warriors and

Ethiopian tribes from east Africa. There is a religious reason for the way Rastafarians let their hair grow: they quote the Bible's invocation: "No razor shall come upon his head" (Numbers 6,5).

Indian influence can also be appreciated in the number of curry dishes in Jamaican cuisine. Curried goat, a popular dish at any Jamaican feast, originated from India. Marijuana also came from India.

Chinese immigrants did not appear on the scene until around 1860. Although the Chinese were few in number, they have risen to prominence in Jamaica. The much-visited national football stadium was designed by Wilson Chong, a Jamaican of Chinese descent.

Some of the minorities play an important role in commercial life. Lebanese, for example, first came to the island at the end of the 19th century, and many stayed on to become small traders. In Jamaica they are known as Syrians, because in the 1890s Lebanon was part of the Ottoman Empire and regarded as part of Syria. Their number and influence have grown considerably over the years. One Lebanese, Edward Seaga, was Prime Minister of Jamaica from 1980 to 1989.

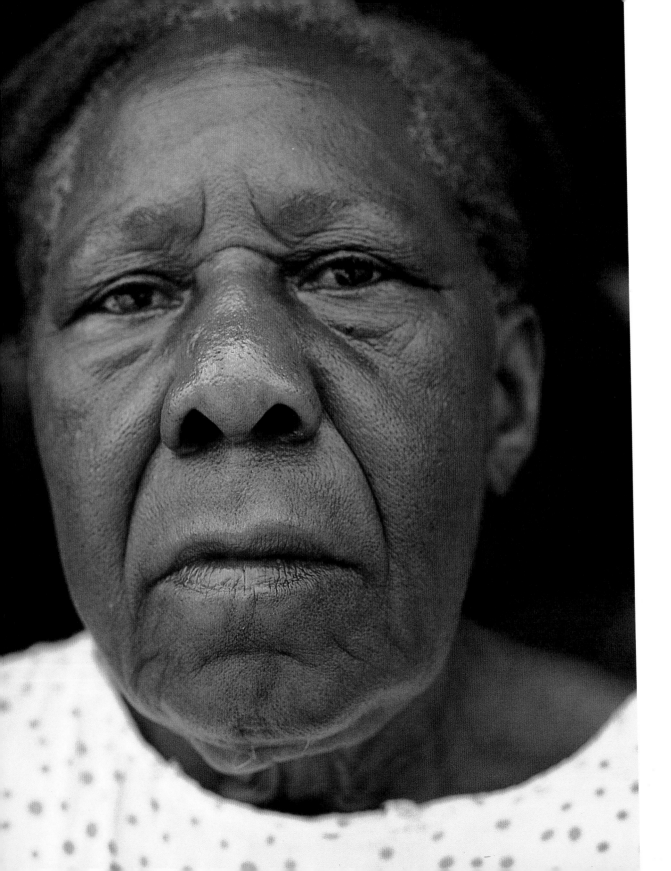

LIFESTYLE

THE PRESENT PATTERNS OF LIFE, be they urban or rural, are directly derived from the plantation society in 18th century Jamaica.

The pace of life is generally laid-back and has been described as "soon-come-ism," a Creole phrase that essentially says: it doesn't really matter much if you put off until tomorrow what doesn't have to be done today.

FAMILY LIFE

Family life in Jamaica, as in many other Caribbean nations, tends to be matriarchial. This means that the mother, rather than the father or both parents together, is the head of the family. The reason for this is historical. Slavery has been abolished for well over 150 years, but the forms and patterns of family life that were created by slavery continue to influence today's society. Under slavery, marriage between slaves was not recognized.

The idea of the father as an integral member of a nuclear family did not exist under slavery, nor for a long time after its abolition. Even today, if a father leaves a family, the children invariably stay with the mother and her extended family.

The woman, then, plays a central and decisive role in the family. She has access to birth control and will have children when *she* wants to. Primary health care clinics provide prenatal and postnatal care for mothers and children.

The tradition of female self-reliance has also been nurtured and sustained by contemporary economic factors. Unemployment is high, and men are often forced to leave their families in order to find work. This is particularly true in rural areas, where a woman will often shoulder the responsibility of bringing up the children. Even in urban areas, a mother and her children's grandmothers will manage the day-to-day family affairs while the husband is away working, perhaps in another country.

George Lamming, a West Indian novelist, succinctly summed up the reality of family life in these memorable words: "my mother who fathered me ... my father who had fathered only the idea of me."

Opposite: **Jamaican woman. Women in Jamaica have a long tradition of strength and self-reliance.**

GROWING UP AND WORKING

The typical Jamaican child grows up with his or her mother and siblings. The father may be a part of the family, but he is more likely to make only occasional visits. He may be working elsewhere, or it may be that he has another, separate family.

Many young school leavers, especially males, drift to Kingston in the hope of finding employment, be it working in a garage or helping a relative at a market stall. An average salary is around $20 a week, and many youngsters change jobs frequently. There is also the lure of traveling overseas to seek employment. Over one million Jamaicans are living overseas, mostly in the United States.

A young female school leaver may seek employment in one of the fields traditionally associated with women: health care and clerical or secretarial work. The 1975 Employment Act guarantees equal pay for equal work. While this is true for jobs in the civil service, women are the first to be dismissed in times of economic depression.

MARRIAGE

Sex before marriage is common and socially acceptable in Jamaica. The distinction between a legitimate and an illegitimate child does not have the same significance as it does in many other societies. The rights of an illegitimate child are protected by law, and there is no social stigma attached to being illegitimate. Illegitimate children are certainly not treated any differently by their parents. It is not unusual to see children acting as ushers and bridesmaids at their parents' wedding.

A pregnant woman below the age of 20 is not unusual, whether married or not. It is also common for people to marry at the age of 40 or 50. Whatever the age of the marriage partners, the event itself is always an occasion for great celebration. Before the event takes place, there is always a formal meeting between the parents and their future in-laws. Presents start arriving long before the actual wedding, sometimes months in advance. Friends or relatives usually send eggs to be used in the wedding cake. Grandmothers traditionally help to choose the clothes for the ceremony.

On the night before the wedding, most of the guests will stay up singing and eating. The church ceremony is an occasion for everyone to dress up in their best clothes.

The church ceremony itself is fairly short and hymns are sung. The ceremony is followed by the cutting of the wedding cake and speeches are made. The happy event ends with a large feast and more merrymaking until the early hours of the morning.

FUNERALS

A funeral, like a marriage, is very much a public event. Grieving for the loss of loved ones is not something confined to the privacy of the home. The coffin is likely to be displayed on the verandah of the family's home, with the face of the deceased revealed by a split in the top of the coffin. Relatives, friends, and neighbors visit to pay their respects, and some join in the loud wailing that expresses the grief of close family members.

There is a tradition that a husband should not see his wife's coffin being placed in the ground. It is believed that if he does and then remarries, his second wife will suffer an early death.

The relative rarity of legal marriages in Jamaica does not mean that people fail to establish lasting unions. The main obstacle is financial constraint. Many men simply cannot afford the expense of a proper wedding and the setting up of a new home.

Jamaica's low death rate reflects the fact that it has a young population. Its low birth rate is the result of family planning programs in the 1970s and 1980s. Young Jamaican women were encouraged with slogans such as: "Plan Your Family. Better Your Life."

LIFESTYLE STATISTICS

Infant Mortality:
11 per thousand (United States: 10 per thousand).

Life Expectancy:
73 years. Males: 71 years. Females: 75 years.

Urban/Rural Distribution:
55% of Jamaica's 2.4 million people live in towns.

Literacy:
73.1% of all Jamaicans can read and write.

Birth Rate:
24 births each year per 1,000 of the population.

Death Rate:
6 deaths each year per 1,000 of the population.

Marriage Rate:
4.5 per 1,000 of the population

Divorce Rate:
0.3 per 1,000 of the population

(Source: *New Internationalist* magazine, 1992)

RURAL LIFE

Rural Jamaica was once a vital part of an economy that was dependent on agriculture, namely sugar and banana exports to the United States and Europe. But prices for these products plunged drastically during the Great Depression, reducing the income of many small farmers. Several hurricanes in the 1930s and imported crop diseases added further difficulties. Young people began to drift from the rural areas to towns in search of employment.

The typical Jamaican farm is less than five acres in size and tends to be self-sufficient. Yams are commonly cultivated, and their underground tubers are eaten for their starch-rich content. Yams are broad-leafed climbing plants; farmers provide stakes for them to grow up on. The tubers are peeled and then boiled or roasted and eaten like potatoes. Yams have a distinctively slimy feel and turn brown fairly quickly if they are not kept in water. In the United States, the yam is sometimes confused with the sweet potato and mistakenly called by the same name.

Other common crops in Jamaica include plantains, mangoes, and cassava. The plantain is a type of banana that, unlike the variety commonly eaten raw in the United States, requires cooking to prepare its hard flesh for consumption.

The small farmer may also keep chickens, pigs, and goats. The farmer sells the surplus fruit, vegetables, and livestock at the local market for cash, and this provides a source of income for rural families.

In rural areas, young children often help their parents with chores such as fetching water from the public tap in the village.

Ghettos are a prominent feature in and outside towns and cities as there is a shortage of affordable housing. The situation is not improving as more and more young people flock to the cities in search of employment.

URBAN GHETTOS

The urban areas of Jamaica continue to grow as more and more people leave the countryside to seek a better life in the cities. This adds to the existing problem of accommodating the island's urban population. In 1975, the government established a housing corporation and trust in an attempt to deal with the influx of low-income families into Kingston and other towns. Low interest loans for improvements to existing dwellings, as well as the financing of new housing programs, are funded by compulsory subscriptions from employers and employees.

The amount of funds such schemes have at their disposal varies with the general state of the economy. Unfortunately, the 1990s are proving to be economically depressed, so ghettos continue to be a feature of urban life. Kingston, in particular, suffers in this respect as thousands live in corrugated-iron shacks. These ghettos are home to Jamaica's many urban

gangs that flourish in the harsh economic climate of deprivation.

Many of the gangs have their origins in the political gangs that were attached to the rival political parties in the 1970s and early 1980s. Since then the gangs have divorced themselves from the politicians, and leadership has passed to Mafia-type bosses involved in the drug underworld.

The powerful gangster leaders are known as "top rankin'" or "mos' wanted." Concern about urban violence surfaced in 1987 after the murder of Peter Tosh, a reggae musician; and in the same year, a high-ranking judge in the Supreme Court was assassinated. In 1992, the slums of the capital were turned into a battleground between rival gangs and the police after 40,000 people attended the funeral of a man alleged to have been involved in one of the more prominent gangs. Over a dozen people died and many were injured. Neighborhood curfews were imposed in an attempt to quell the disorder.

In her own little corner of a teeming city, this fruit and vegetable seller needs only the wall of a building against which to lean her cases and a small table, and she's ready for business.

On the corner of King and Duke Streets in modern Kingston.

LIFE IN KINGSTON

Because Jamaica is a small island, its capital, Kingston, plays a bigger part in the lives of Jamaicans than does London, for example, in the lives of the British or Washington, D.C., in the lives of Americans. Kingston is a mecca for young people who flock there hoping to find fame and fortune as the world's next reggae star, but too often lucky if they find any work at all. Most of the country's important social, artistic, and national events take place in the capital.

There is demarcation between the affluent minority, who aspire to a North American lifestyle and live in the surrounding foothills and suburbs, and the majority, who have low income jobs or no regular employment. Yet, as many social commentators have noted, it is the economically least-advantaged parts of the city that provide a cultural dynamic that spills over to the rest of the country.

The government has made some efforts to improve the living conditions of these disadvantaged groups. One of the more famous areas of Kingston is Tivoli Gardens. Once a slum area known as Back o' Wall, it was transformed into a lively community with the establishment of a health clinic, a maternity center, and numerous recreational facilities. Its carefully painted murals point to its youth and their cultural energy.

Schoolboys taking a break between classes.

EDUCATION

For a long time, only the privileged white children in Jamaica had access to the private schools run by various churches. Since independence, great efforts have been made by the government to provide universal education. Presently, education is free for all children aged 6 to 15. This is the result of a ten-year education plan achieved with financial aid from the World Bank, the United States, and Canada.

FORMAL EDUCATION Kindergartens prepare children for entry into more formal schooling. The government pays the teachers' salaries, but it is up to each parish to provide suitable buildings. Around 90% of all eligible Jamaican children go to elementary school. Just over half of all those who are eligible attend high school, as the dropout rate increases dramatically after the age of 12 or 13.

In many countries of the Caribbean, education tends to be shaped by the colonial power that ruled the nation. In Jamaica, the influence of the

Schoolboys taking a break between classes.

Girls have equal opportunities to obtain an education. Many do extremely well and go on to further their studies, either at the University of West Indies or at overseas universities.

British educational system can still be discerned. The language of instruction is English, and shortly after the age of 10, children sit for an examination. Based on the results of this examination, some children are selected for entry to prestigious government-aided high schools. The majority of children, however, transfer to their local comprehensive (junior high) school where, at the end of the third year, placement tests determine which set of examinations they will take.

The main academic examination is the British General Certificate of Education at Ordinary Level (GCE "O" levels), taken at the age of 15 or 16. Besides the British certificate, there are various other examinations organized by the Caribbean Examination Council that offer technical and commercial certification.

At 18, the more academically inclined students take the GCE Advanced Level examination. Success ensures entry into college. Less than 3% of Jamaican students take the "A" Level examination. Unless a student was selected for a high school at the age of 10, or transferred there later from a comprehensive school, he or she is unlikely to take this examination.

VOCATIONAL AND HIGHER EDUCATION There are also vocational schools where skills like carpentry, metalwork, and home economics are taught. Jamaica has nine teacher-training colleges, a College of Agriculture, a College of Arts, and a Cultural Training Center specializing in arts, music, and dancing. Graduates of these colleges are recognized as specialist teachers of their chosen subject.

Jamaica is home to one of the three campuses of the University of the West Indies founded in 1948. The other two campuses are located in Barbados and Trinidad. The Jamaican campus is situated just outside Kingston. It started with just 32 medical students and now boasts a student population of over 8,000. It attracts students not only from Jamaica but also from smaller neighboring islands in the Caribbean that cannot support their own university. During the 1970s, the University of the West Indies was at the forefront of an intellectual movement that stressed the need for Jamaicans and other West Indians to discover their own cultural and historical roots. Research, publications, and courses were designed to redress the imbalance caused by centuries of European domination.

THE UNDER- AND OVERPRIVILEGED Adult illiteracy was a major problem facing the country after independence. The Jamaican Movement for the Advancement of Literacy (JAMAL) has been successfully combating this drawback. In the last 20 years, more than a quarter million Jamaicans have enrolled in classes organized by JAMAL.

Finally, at the other end of the educational spectrum, there are private schools in Jamaica for the benefit of wealthy families. These tend to be denominational, with a large number of expatriate teachers. Some wealthy Jamaicans also send their children abroad for education, mostly to the United States.

Education in Jamaica is compulsory and free for children aged between 6 and 15. Of all Jamaicans over the age of 25, some 19% have no schooling, over 75% have completed the first level, over 5% the second level, and 0.5% have post-secondary education.

The *Cannabis sativa* plant, better known as ganja in Jamaica.

MARIJUANA

The smoking of marijuana, known as ganja ("GAN-jah") in Jamaica, is very much a part of the lifestyle for young people, especially young males. The plant is not native to the Caribbean but was introduced by Indian laborers imported in the last century.

It is illegal to smoke ganja, but it is understandable if a visitor to the country thinks otherwise. It is commonly found among the audience at sporting events or in cinemas, and Rastafarians smoke it at their religious rituals. Many consider it to be a general tonic and add it to their tea and cake batter.

Thousands of Jamaicans are employed in the preparation, growing, and harvesting of marijuana in the more remote rural regions of the country. Most of the harvest is flown to the United States from the numerous illegal airstrips scattered around the island. The authorities have tried to clamp down on these activities, but in a country where there is high unemployment and low wages, the temptation to get rich by cultivating ganja is great. It

is common knowledge that professionals and otherwise respectable figures are also involved in the business as there are large profits to be made by exporting the crop to the United States. In the early 1980s, *Newsweek* came to the conclusion that only Colombia provided more of the drug for U.S. consumption than Jamaica.

Official attitudes toward the use of the drug have varied over the last 30 years. Shortly after independence, a law was passed whereby anyone caught growing the plant could be imprisoned, but this law has since been repealed. Various proposals have been made to legalize the drug for personal use so that ganja would be seen as just another crop, like tobacco for cigarettes or hops for beer. Thus, it is believed, the price of ganja would fall and little profit would be made in pursuing its cultivation, thereby decreasing it.

In the meantime, ganja continues to be illegal, and the police continue to try and clamp down on the export trade by raiding farms and closing down private airstrips where large quantities are flown out. The maximum sentence for the cultivation of ganja is a fine of up to $1,120 or a jail sentence of up to 10 years or both.

RELIGION

WHEN THE SLAVES were brought into Jamaica from Africa, they were not allowed to practice their own religion. This was not simply because the slave owners believed Christianity was spiritually more meaningful, but because a policy of religious intolerance was one way of breaking down the cultural identity that united slaves in the face of oppression. Christianity also taught the Africans to reject their original beliefs and to accept their new subservience with humility.

African religions did not, however, die out so easily. Missionaries found it was far easier to convert the slaves if they adapted some traditional African beliefs and incorporated them into their teachings. The slaves accepted Christianity at face value but used it as a way of continuing to practice their own rituals. Nowadays, Christianity flourishes in a variety of forms alongside other faiths that represent a hybrid of Christianity and African animism. Jamaica's own unique religion is Rastafarianism.

There are also small communities of Jews, Hindus, and Moslems.

Above: **An Anglican church in Falmouth.**

Opposite: **A river baptism for adult Jamaicans.**

CHRISTIAN FAITHS

About 75% of Jamaicans claim to be Christians. In some countries where other beliefs existed before Christianity was introduced, the people have adapted the church service to suit these earlier practises. A typical church service in Jamaica involves a high degree of audience participation. Music is nearly always provided by means of an electronic organ or a tambourine, and singing can break out spontaneously.

A Christian cemetery in Newcastle.

There are more than 100 Christian denominations in Jamaica, the majority of which are Protestant; most Protestant Jamaicans belong to the Baptist, Methodist, or Anglican communities. The Baptists first came to Jamaica in the 1780s, after the American War of Independence. Baptists and Methodists were instrumental in converting large numbers of slaves. They were particularly successful because of their objection to the practice of slavery and their willingness to support the campaign for its abolition. The first Methodist missionary, the Reverend Coke, arrived on the island in 1789, but the Coke chapel was closed down the following year by the authorities, who objected to the political implications of his work with slaves.

There are also a host of smaller groups including the Seventh-Day Adventists, the Church of God, and the United Church of Christ.

Roman Catholicism, which arrived with the first Spanish conquerors, is found mainly among sections of the Chinese and Indian populations.

In recent years, Jamaica has seen the rising popularity of Christian fundamentalist groups, most of which came to the island from America. Many of the sects place strong emphasis on gospel singing and powerful sermonizing that admonishes the faithless and celebrates the rewards of the new faith.

ANIMISM

Animism is a belief based on the idea that animals, plants, and even inanimate objects have souls. The word itself comes from the Latin word *anima*, meaning "soul." The main belief of animism is that spiritual beings are capable of influencing human events. Animistic religions came to Jamaica with the African slaves, and despite being banned by the European powers, they have never completely disappeared from Jamaica's spiritual landscape.

This African heritage is most apparent in the spirit cults that continue to attract some believers in Jamaica. *Kumina* ("KOO-mi-nah") is the name of one of the most important of these cults. Worshipers invoke their own deceased family members and the spirits that are called *zombies*. The process of calling up an ancestral spirit relies heavily on drum music that helps create the necessary trance-like state. Two types of drums are employed: the *kimbanda* ("kim-BAHN-dah"), a large drum covered with goat skin that produces a bass sound, and the *plain kyas* ("kee-yahs"),

In rituals associated with animism, the participant is often in a trance and therefore does not feel pain when stepping on broken glass and other sharp objects.

which is much smaller than the bass drum and produces a treble sound associated with the calling up of a spirit. The use of music and dance is part of a Congolese cult.

The main *kumina* ritual is still acted out on the island, although only occasionally. It is very dramatic. The drums used in the ceremony are showered with alcohol, and the chief priestess sings a hymn and performs a ritual performed by the original African communities centuries ago. The priestess, who is known as Miss Quennie, is credited with special spiritual powers that put her in a trance and enable her to communicate with the spirits. The sacrifice of an animal, usually a goat, is also a part of the ritual.

Kumina is bound up with the use of *obeah* ("OH-be-uh"), a form of witchcraft that uses special herbs and roots as well as concoctions made from blood, feathers, and bones to make and cast spells. *Obeah* can be seen as black magic and is allied to voodooism.

Although *kumina* is banned by the government, it continues to exist in a surreptitious way. Some people still turn to it in the belief that spiritual forces can cure illnesses and harm enemies. Ordinarily, the animistic element in Jamaican religious beliefs reveals itself only in popular superstition. The "rollin' calf" is one of the spirits in Jamaican folklore that has the habit of traveling during the night, dragging a chain with it. Farm animals, it is believed, may be killed by it. One common protective device is a bottle hung from a nearby tree.

POCOMANIA

So prevalent and significant is the influence of animism in Jamaica that it reaches beyond the practice of the original African rituals of *kumina* and *obeah* to produce a unique kind of Christianity. Where Christianity has merged with animistic beliefs, the resulting faith is known as Pocomania. Adherents meet to participate in a ceremony with the hope that they will be possessed by the spirit of God. The dialect word for the cult is "puckamenna" and the religious dancing is described as "dancing the puckoo."

The altar of the traditional Christian service is replaced by a long table covered with a white cloth upon which bowls and plates of food are illuminated by candles. The almighty spirit is then invoked through song and dance. Evangelistic preaching is followed by chanting and the singing of hymns. Powerful rhythms encourage the congregation to join in to attain a state of grace. Members of the congregation leave their places to begin a slow dancing march around the table, led by the leader, who is addressed as "the shepherd" if a male, "mother" if female. Possession by a spirit is marked by a frenzied level of singing or groaning, or perhaps by speaking in tongues. Pocomanians believe that after such a possession, the spirit remains with the person as a kind of guardian angel who can then be consulted for advice and guidance.

The Revival Zion sect is a smaller offshoot of the merging of Christianity with animism, and it shares many characteristics of Pocomania, such as preaching and dancing to the sound of music.

The Pocomanian altar is laden with offerings of flowers, candles, and food.

The Ethiopian Emperor Haile Selassie in 1968.

RASTAFARIANISM

Rastafarianism is a quasi-Christian religion that draws inspiration from the Book of Revelations, the speeches of Haile Selassie I, the Old Testament, the prophecies of Marcus Garvey, and the lyrics of reggae musicians Bob Marley, Peter Tosh, and Bunny Walker. Although Rastafarians believe that their religion has no "origin" (it has always existed), it is generally agreed that Marcus Garvey, the man who stressed the automony of black consciousness, was of pivotal importance in the growth of Rastafarianism.

Garvey was born in St. Ann's Bay, Jamaica, in 1887 and grew up in a society based on color differences. When Garvey left Jamaica for the United States in 1916, he was reported to have said, "Look to Africa when a black king shall be crowned; he shall be your Redeemer." Also, the Bible refers to Ethiopia more than 40 times, and some claimed that Ethopia was the "earthly paradise." Thus, when Haile Selassie was crowned emperor of Ethiopia in 1930, the prophecy was seen to have been fulfilled. Haile Selassie was seen as the black reincarnated Christ. The word "Rastafarianism" comes from Selassie's title before he was crowned emperor—Ras Tafari, which means "crown prince" in Amharic, the main language of Ethiopia.

In the years following Garvey's death, Leonard Howell established a collective in Jamaica for over 1,500 followers. The most distinctive physical feature of the Rastafarians began to emerge: the "dreadlocks" hairstyle that boldly proclaimed their Africanness.

Rastafarians, or Rastas as they are often called, believe in the ubiquity and divinity of Jah Rasta, the spirit who "dwells with us all." They believe this spirit will help oppressed people to a heaven on earth. Rastafarians observe dietary laws similiar to those of the Jews. Many items, like pork, are excluded from their diet. Milk and coffee are also avoided, and many do not drink alcohol. As with nearly all the other religious communities in Jamaica, Rastafarians integrate music into their faith. Reggae music and lyrics actually developed within a Rastafarian context and produced the famous reggae star Bob Marley.

Kumasi, an internationally known reggae singer, sports the dreadlocks that are the mark of the Rastafarian religion.

Three sects of the religion are to be found in Jamaica. The oldest and most traditional group is recognizable by the long cloaks of its members and their habit of having their hair rolled into turbans. They live in small communities that try to be as economically self-sufficient as possible. A second group, known as the Twelve Tribes, is most famous for having Bob Marley as one of its members. It is characterized by a stronger political element than the older group and champions the cause of working class Jamaicans. A third group is the Ethiopian Zion Coptic Church. This sect is looked down on by many members of the other two sects, partly because of its willingness to engage in the commercial distribution of marijuana.

The number of Rastafarians worldwide is estimated to be more than one million and it remains a vibrant religious force in Jamaica. Although the religion has spread to other islands in the Caribbean and to communities in the United Kingdom and the United States, the dynamism of the religion continues to be based on a strong sense of African pride.

LANGUAGE

ENGLISH IS THE OFFICIAL LANGUAGE of Jamaica, a legacy of the island having been a part of the British Empire. When slaves were brought from Africa, they were forced to learn the language of their masters.

ENGLISH HERITAGE

English was spoken with the intonation and speech patterns of the slaves' native tongue. Sounds that did not exist in their native African languages were naturally difficult to pronounce, so the nearest equivalent was adopted. This was the case with, for example, the "th" sound; thus "the" became "de," "then" became "den," and "that" became "dat."

Since communication between the English masters and slaves was limited to issuing orders and conveying basic information, the slaves simplified and adapted the language accordingly. Over a period of time, this gave rise to a very distinctive patois ("PAH-twah"), the name given to local dialect.

It is not just the pronunciation that makes Jamaican patois so distinctive. The vocabulary used suggests that the islanders have been caught in a time warp, preserving words and phrases found only in the works of Shakespeare or the Bible. Saying goodbye to a friend might produce the 17th century phrase, "Peradventure I wi' see you tomorrow" (Perhaps I will see you tomorrow). Jamaicans speak of insects that "biteth like the serpent" or of a court decision they approve of as a "righteous one."

Opposite and below: **Although English is the official language in Jamaica, the grammar and pronunciation of words are adapted from various African languages.**

81

A JAMAICAN GLOSSARY

Words

belly-god	glutton	Merica	America
bredda	brother	mi	me, I
brekfus	breakfast	mistress	married woman
chile	child	nyam	eat, food
dawta	daughter	ongle	only
deh	is, are	pickney	child
de	the	sinting	something
fah	for	teck	take
faisty	rude, impertinent	teef	steal
liad	liar	quashie	fool
mash	destroy	wakgud	goodbye
maskita	mosquito	(walk good)	

Phrases

"Everyt'ubf kool, mon? Everyt'ing irie?"
"Are you feeling good?"

"Cuss-cuss never bore hole in skin."
"Sticks and stones may break my bones but words will never hurt me."

Jamaicans are educated in Standard English and the Jamaican paper *Daily Gleaner* uses Standard English. In conversation, however, Standard English is mixed with colloquial words and expressions. The different language levels reflect the social levels of Jamaican society—the higher the level, the greater its use of Standard English.

Generally speaking, while the outsider may not understand every word of an English dialogue between two Jamaicans on the street, their meaning can still be discerned. Casual conversation among friends and family members involves the full range of Jamaican English, where pronunciation, vocabulary, and grammar depart radically from Standard English. For example, "Di kuk di tel mi faamin, bot it nat so" means "The cook told me I was pretending to be sick, but it's not so." The main verb in this sentence, "faamin," comes from the English word "form," but has its own meaning of "to pretend."

JAMAICAN GRAMMAR

The English used by the slaves was influenced by the grammatical structures of their native African languages. Different relationships between nouns in an English sentence, for example, are expressed by the use of different pronouns ("I," "me," and "my"), but in Jamaican grammar, "me" performs this function all the time. For instance, "I feel happy" becomes "Me happy" and "My book is lost" becomes "Me book lost."

What grammarians call "case" has also changed in Jamaican English. Take the example of "he," "him," and "his." The sentence "I kicked *him*" uses the objective case because "him" is the object of the sentence. "I kicked *his* ball" uses the genitive case because the ball belongs to the object. "*He* went home" uses the nominative case because "he" is the subject of the sentence. In Jamaican English, all three of these sentences would use "him": "I kicked *him*," "I kicked *him* ball," and "*Him* went home."

The *dem* tag is used to indicate a plural in Jamaican grammar: "de boy dem" means "the boys." One exception to this rule is the word "I", which is used twice ("I and I") to indicate "we."

Jamaican Creole developed not as a language of defeated or depressed people, but one of a people with a strong sense of the ridiculous, a gift for vivid imagery, earthy humor, and bawdy curses.

LANGUAGE AND NATIONAL PRIDE

Until recently, Jamaican English only existed in the form of an oral tradition known as Jamaican Talk. It hardly ever appeared in print, and when it did it was usually ridiculed or condescendingly called "quaint." Yet it was the means of communication and expression for the majority of Jamaicans.

Before independence, there was social pressure to speak Standard English because it was seen as the norm, and any departure from it was regarded as a deviation or an abberation. This unrealistic expectation fostered an inferiority complex in the majority of Jamaicans who could not speak Standard English. It was most damaging when Jamaicans had to deal with the British administration. In a court of law, for instance, they were expected to speak as close to Standard English as possible. But as defendants struggled to communicate in a language they were uncomfortable with, the clarity of their presentation suffered as a result of nervousness and insecurity. Naturally, their case in court was weakened.

With independence and the growth of national consciousness, there is a new pride in Jamaican English. The reggae musician Bob Marley played a significant role in this process because his international concert tours brought Jamaican English into prominence. His gift of expressing ideas and emotions in Jamaican English has done enormous service to what was previously looked down on as "broken English." Dub poetry, or poetry in Jamaican English, also shows that Jamaican Talk can be written.

Academics have argued that Jamaican Creole should be recognized as a separate language. They point out that, historically, it has evolved separately from English. Jamaican Creole is not promoted for simply linguistic reasons, but for nationalistic and political purposes as well. Some people in Jamaica reason that Standard English is the language of a small elite and therefore excludes the majority of citizens from fully participating in their society.

Jamaican Talk is characterized by irony, satire, and ridicule. Those not familiar with it may find it disconcerting, but they soon realize that sarcasm is used not only against others but against oneself.

TWO LANGUAGES?

Standard English will always be used because of its economic importance for international commerce. To abandon English would cut Jamaica off from the international community. At the same time, Jamaican Creole allows Jamaicans to express their national and cultural identity with pride and a sense of history.

In addition, there is a Caribbean form of Standard English that represents a compromise between the two linguistic traditions. Caribbean English is increasingly popular and accepted in schools and by employers.

Young people growing up in Jamaica use Jamaican Creole at home and Caribbean English in school and the workplace. Yet many aspire to be proficient in Standard English as it is associated with success and prestige.

THE ARTS

IN THE EARLY YEARS, the effort to strive for a unique aesthetic identity was led by artists and writers from the educated upper class. But the situation was changed in the 1940s, when prominent artists and writers fueled a movement toward fostering national pride in the arts.

DANCE AND MUSIC

Dance, music, and song are not easily separated as they have a common origin in Jamaican folktales and tradition.

The *mento* is the most traditional dance in Jamaica. Mento refers to the dance as well as to the music and the words. Musicians beat out the tune on bongo drums and the rhumba box, an instrument adapted from the African thumb piano, while singers recount past tales. The Jamaican quadrille is a folk dance that was brought to the island by Europeans, then adapted by Jamaicans who added African elements.

Calypso, a jazz-influenced style of music that originated in Trinidad, is especially popular in tourist areas where it accompanies limbo dancers.

A truly Jamaican part of the island's music are worksongs that date back to the days when slaves made up songs to relieve boredom and hardship. The songs are characterized by short lyrical lines that are repeated. African influence can be detected in the alternation of lines between a lead singer and a chorus. But unlike the call-and-response routine in African spirituals, worksongs are not spiritual in nature or function. They also differ from the traditional black spirituals of the southern United States in that, instead of soulful melancholy, there is optimism and a workaday atmosphere.

Above: The limbo, a dance where the dancer bends his body backwards to pass under a horizontal pole, is usually accompanied by calypso music. The professional limbo dancer is able to bend back so far that he can clear a horizontal pole placed at knee level.

Opposite: **Rastafarian carving in a tree trunk.**

Statue of the legendary Bob Marley outside his home in Kingston. Marley's house is now a museum.

REGGAE MUSIC

The most distinctive and exciting music of Jamaica is the reggae sound that first emerged in the early 1970s. But the origins of this music go back at least a decade before that, when Jamaican musicians invented ska music—a blend of rhythm and blues (R&B) and mento music. R&B introduced the electric guitar and organ, which later became important instruments in reggae.

It is not certain where the term *reggae* came from, perhaps from the patois *streggae* (rudeness or rude-boy) or *regge-regge* (quarrel). It may also be a purely descriptive term, meaning simply "regular," as the music does have a regular, almost hypnotic, bass-dominated sound.

The lyrics of reggae music point to its street origins. Nearly all the early practitioners of reggae music came from the slum areas of Kingston, and their songs voiced the concerns of a dissatisfied African-Jamaican youth that were ignored by the established authorities. In the 1970s, reggae music was not played on Jamaican radio because of this political element and its association with "rude-boy" music. The music also has a strong Rastafarian influence that emphasizes peace, love, and reconciliation.

Bob Marley became reggae's superstar partly because of his superior musicianship and partly because of his ethical stance towards political turmoil within Jamaica and toward the war in Vietnam. Another international success from Jamaica was Desmond Dekker, who had a big success with his songs "The Israelites" and "Toots and the Mayals."

JIMMY CLIFF
(1948–)

With the sole exception of Bob Marley, Jimmy Cliff is the best known Jamaican singer and songwriter. He combines traditional reggae with a soul element to give his music a very distinctive sound.

Cliff's introduction to the music business was by way of a song he wrote about an ice-cream parlor and a record store in Jamaica. One of the owners of the store was so impressed by the song that he entered the record business and signed up Cliff. That was in 1962. Cliff was only 14 years old and living in near poverty. Two years later, he was touring the United States with such hits as "Hurricane Hattie" and "Miss Jamaica." In 1969, his "Wonderful World, Beautiful People" was a big hit on both sides of the Atlantic.

In 1973, Cliff reached a wider audience after starring in the film *The Harder They Come*. The film tells the story of a boy from the Jamaican countryside who goes to the capital city to look for employment but falls into bad company. The film was an international success and introduced reggae music to the rest of the world because it included a cross-section of some of the best reggae songs, including "Sitting in Limbo" by Cliff himself, "Rivers of Babylon" sung by The Lemodians, and "Shanty Town" sung by Desmond Dekker. Cliff appeared in the movies *Bongo Man* (1980) and *Club Paradise* (1986).

BOB MARLEY (1945–1981)

Marley was born in 1945 of mixed-race parentage. When he was 12 years old, he moved with his African-Jamaican mother to the Trenchtown ghetto in Kingston. Three years later, he formed his first band. When he was 17, he met Jimmy Cliff and made his first record, "Judge Not," with his group called the Wailing Wailers. In 1967, the group set up their own record label, and their first major success was "Trench Town Rock," which was number one in Jamaica for five months in 1971.

By then the band was known as the Wailers, and they began touring in Britain and the United States. Several of Marley's own compositions at this time were big hits by other artists, the most well known being "I Shot the Sheriff" by Eric Clapton and "Guava Jelly" by Barbra Streisand. Despite the international success that Marley and the Wailers enjoyed, their roots remained in Jamaica and with Rastafarianism.

The political violence that rocked Jamaica in the 1970s saw an attempt on Marley's life in 1976, but he recovered and continued his career. In 1980, Marley collapsed on stage and died eight months later from cancer of the brain. He was 36 years old.

Despite his wealth and fame, Marley never forgot his ghetto roots and returned to them in what is probably his most famous song, "No Woman, No Cry."

Said I remember when we used to sit
In the government yard in Trenchtown
Observing all the hypocrites
Mingle with the good people we meet …
And then Georgie would make the fire light,
I seh, log wood burnin' thru the nights
Then we would cook cornmeal porridge,
Of which I'd share with you …

The Jamaican government organized a state funeral that was attended by thousands; the funeral procession stretched for 55 miles. The government also commissioned a statue of the star to stand outside the National Gallery.

LITERATURE

In 1949 Victor Reid published his novel *New Day.* For the first time, there was an attempt to explore what it meant to be a Jamaican, as opposed to being a lost citizen of Africa or a European living in Jamaica. But more significantly, the novel was written in Jamaican dialect, and this opened the world of novels to the ordinary Jamaican.

The importance of the right language to reach Jamaican readers is reflected in the dedication a writer, Ken Maxwell, made in one of his books: "to all Jamaicans who have found that nowhere else in the world is real English spoken …" Jamaican English presents vivid impressions and moods that are instantly recognized by Jamaicans, and it gives them an empathy with the characters of a story in a way that Standard English often does not.

Other important Jamaican novelists include Roger Mais and Andrew Salkey. Earlier writers like Mais and Salkey left Jamaica for Britain and never returned to live in their own country. Salkey wrote several novels, but he also wrote stories for children, including *Hurricane, Earthquake, Drought,* and *Riot.*

An interesting aspect of Mais's development as a writer is that he only became a novelist in the last three years of his life. Born in 1905, Mais wrote only poetry and short stories until 1953, when his novel *The Hills Were Joyful Together* was greeted with critical acclaim. The following year he published *Brother Man,* and in 1955, the year he died, *Black Lightning.* All three books are grim sociological studies of poverty and prison life, and are highly regarded.

Mais's books had a great influence on another gifted writer, John Hearne. Hearne's novels, which include *Voices Under the Window* and *The Autumn Equinox,* have been described as sensitive and powerful.

Jamaican literature only emerged in the 20th century. Few Jamaicans were taught to read and write, and so the audience for literary works was a small one.

Miss Louise Bennett of Jamaica, affectionally called Miss Lou, has done much for Jamaican language and folk culture.

DUB POETRY

Dub poetry has been called "the baby of reggae." Although its emergence is associated with the 1970s, its roots can be traced in the work of Louise Bennett. Louise Bennett, who is known as "Miss Lou," has written poems for over 30 years using authentic Jamaican English that ensures her audience, regardless of their social class, can appreciate and enjoy her poems. Her poetry is firmly rooted in Jamaica's oral folk tradition, and she claims inspiration from the Bible and the folk songs of Jamaica.

Louise Bennett's poems first appeared in Jamaica's newspaper, but they are designed to be read aloud and turned into a performance. The subject of her poetry is life in modern Jamaica, ranging from topics like public events, street life, and politics.

"MI CYAAN BELIEVE IT" BY MICHAEL SMITH

Mi seh mi cyaan believe it	I'm saying I can't believe it
Mi seh mi cyaan believe it	I'm saying I can't believe it
room dem a rent	rooms for rent
mi apply within	so I applied within
but as me go in	but as I went in
cockroach rat an scorpion	a cockroach, rat, and a
also come in	scorpion also came in
waan good	it wasn't good
nose haffi run	I knew I had to run
but me naw go sideung	but I can't go and sit upon
pan igh wall	the wall
like Humpty Dumpty	like Humpty Dumpty
mi a face me reality	I have to face reality

When Louise Bennett first began writing poems, she was looked down upon as someone who could only write broken English. In fact, when her first anthology appeared in 1966, a glossary of four pages was needed to help non-Jamaicans understand her. Now she is a national figure, highly appreciated for her pioneering role in the vibrant contemporary culture.

Louise Bennett has inspired new dub poets like Michael Smith, Mutabaruka, Linton Kwesi Johnson, and Oku Onora. These poets, many of whom have had a university education, consciously turned away from Standard English to write in Jamaican English. Linton Kwesi Johnson describes their poetry in these terms: "Here the spoken/chanted word is the dominant mode. People's speech and popular music are combined with the Jamaican folk culture and the reggae tradition ... as sources of inspiration and frames of reference."

A good example of dub poetry is Michael Smith's poem "Mi Cyaan Believe It" (I Can't Believe It). Like other dub poets, Smith composed his poems orally and then transcribed them into Jamaican English.

ART

The earliest form of art in Jamaica, painted by Arawak Indians, is found on the walls of caves. It is all that is left of the island's earliest inhabitants. Historians speculate that Arawak art had some influence on the Spanish artists who carved and decorated the friezes found in the buildings of the first capital at St. Ann's Bay.

It was well into the 20th century before any attention was paid to non-European art in Jamaica. The awakening to the influence that African heritage has had on the arts came from the elite of Jamaican society. One such person is the sculptress, Edna Manley, who focused on themes that identified with Jamaican consciousness.

Today, popular art is drawn freely on the walls of buildings in Kingston's Tivoli Gardens area. The locality is considered a ghetto, but artistically it is rich in color and inspiration. It resembles a giant canvas where colors are splashed generously across the walls and yet integrated into a semi-abstract theme. Pictorial subject matter often includes tropical landscapes and the flora and fauna of the island.

EDNA MANLEY

Edna Manley is a talented sculptress whose wood carvings capture indigenous forms. They were seen as inferior and outrageous when they were first exhibited in 1936. But she was undaunted by criticism and continued to focus attention on Jamaican rather than imported values of aesthetic beauty.

Working with Robert Verity and the Institute of Jamaica in the 1940s, Edna Manley was able to organize art lessons for young people at a price they could afford. Eventually, this led to the establishment of the Jamaica School of Art in 1950.

Edna Manley was a major influence on Jamaican art as she was ideally placed to establish a liaison between politics and art. She was married to the late Norman Manley, who founded the People's National Party, and is the mother of former Prime Minister Michael Manley.

"The great thing was to be able to see ourselves as Jamaicans in Jamaica and try to free ourselves from the domination of English aesthetics."

—Edna Manley

In recent years, a number of untaught artists have gained attention because their style is similar to other intuitive artists working in different communities around the world. Loosely grouped together as "primitive" artists, some of these more famous painters include Ralph Campbell, John Dunkley and Mallica Reynolds (the last artist painting under the pseudonym Kapo). While Reynolds is a Pocomanian and the others are Rastafarians, there is no unifying philosophy to their work, and new styles continue to emerge.

Jamaica's National Gallery houses the work of many of the island's most significant artists: landscapes by Ralph Campbell, realistic scenes of everyday life by David Pottinger, and abstract paintings by Eugene Hyde.

LEISURE

SPORTS ARE POPULAR as leisure activities, attracting both participants and spectators of all ages and social classes. Ball games ranging from basketball and netball to cricket and football are very popular with young people. A large sports event, especially an international cricket match, will attract thousands of spectators. Men usually make up most of the crowd, but families are often seen enjoying a picnic at these sports events.

Jamaica is blessed with many sandy beaches, and a day at the seaside is always a popular outing for friends or families. Away from the beaches, dominoes is a popular game and, like the game of chess, attracts its own dedicated players and spectators. Most Jamaican children are introduced to the game in school. There are special facilities for playing dominoes in most Jamaican community areas.

Opposite: **The game of dominoes is very popular among Jamaicans.**

Below: **Cricket is a national sport.**

STORYTELLING

Storytelling has always played an important role in Jamaican culture. During the 18th and 19th centuries, any overt demonstration of the slaves' African heritage was forbidden, and in time, only the remnants of activities such as games and dances survived.

Storytelling was an exception because it could be carried on in the privacy of the slaves' huts. In this way, the stories from Africa were passed down from one generation to another. The most popular stories are those concerning Anansi, the spider man, and these stories often have a moral.

A successful recital of an Anansi tale is theatrical in nature, and nuances of Jamaican patois are used to bring the story alive. Often, a story has key phrases repeated in a certain rhythm that adds drama to the story.

There are also stories about the days when men and women toiled for meager wages in the fields or on the quaysides weighing bananas and loading them onto the waiting boats.

With the advent of television, the art of storytelling is in danger of being lost. But poet Louise Bennett has done much to revive this leisure art form. For years, she traveled across the island staging recitals, performances, and puppet shows to depict these traditional stories. In recent years, the government has recognized the importance of the oral tradition and encouraged its development.

ANANSI TALES

Anansi is cunning and witty, a survivor who is forced to live by his wits in order to cope with demanding circumstances. When luck is running his way he is a man, but when fate takes a turn for the worst and the future looks bleak, Anansi transforms into a spider and conceals himself in his web on the ceiling. A typical tale often ends with the words, "Jack mandora me no chose none," which means "I'm not responsible for the lies I've been telling."

The African origin of the Anansi tales is evident when Anansi encounters animals like tigers, elephants, and monkeys. These animals are not found in the Caribbean, and their presence in a tale betrays its African origin.

FOLK SONGS AND SPIRITUALS

Worksongs were mentioned in the previous chapter. These and church songs are two examples of how Jamaicans integrate their enjoyment of rhythm into their daily lives.

One of the best loved folk songs of Jamaica is "Day Dah Light" ("Day Is Dawning"), also known as "Mr Tallyman" or "Banana Boat Song." Before Harry Belafonte made it popular in the 1960s, the song was sung by women who had been working on the wharf all night loading ships with bananas. The women carried the heavy bunches of bananas on their heads. As they approached the ship, they called out to the tally-man who kept count of the bananas they carried. ("Tally" refers to a piece of wood scored with notches for the items of an account, then split into halves so each party keeps a record of the transaction.) The procession continued until daybreak when the women returned home to their children.

Jamaicans do not sing only about their hardships. There are folk songs that bring out the failings and folly of human nature and the many dimensions of life.

Jamaicans also love to sing spirituals and revivalist songs. These songs reveal the Jamaican belief that there is life after death and that the spirit world is not separate and remote from the world of the living.

EXCERPT FROM "DAY DAH LIGHT"

Day oh, day oh
Day dah light an' me wan' to go home
Day oh, day oh
Day dah light an' me wan' to go home
Come Mr Tallyman, come tally me bananas
Day dah light an' me wan' to go home.

The West Indies at the Oval stadium, 1939. Jamaica's cricket legend George Headley reaches to hit a ball from the English cricket team.

SUPERBOWL—JAMAICA STYLE

The English introduced cricket to Jamaica in the middle of the 19th century. At the time, the game was very much associated with the English upper classes, but it soon caught on with all sections of Jamaican society. For a long time, however, national teams were not chosen simply on merit but sometimes along social and racial lines. It was not until the 1960s that color prejudice ceased to play any part in the selection of teams.

The prestigious international games of cricket are known as test matches and involve eight teams: the West Indies, England, Australia, New Zealand, India, Pakistan, Sri Lanka, and South Africa. A single test match is spread out over a number of days, five or six days being the average.

Jamaicans invariably have a strong presence on the West Indies team. When a test match is in progress, business in Jamaica can be brought to a halt. An intense national pride is generated. The 12,000 seats at the main

JAMAICA'S GREATEST CRICKETERS

During the 1970s, the West Indies team was the clear favorite for every test match it played, but this would not have been the case without Jamaica's Michael Holding (right). For years he was the world's fastest cricket bowler, and his ability to send the ball spinning in high toward the batsman's face was *the* test of any batsman's nerves.

Another all-time great is George Alphonso Headley (opposite). He was born in Panama to a Jamaican mother who brought him up in Jamaica. He first began to play cricket in the early 1920s. He holds the distinction of being the only player to score 200 runs at Lords in London, the Yankee Stadium of international cricket.

A fast-paced bowler can send the ball hurtling towards the batsman at a speed of over 90 miles an hour.

cricket ground are sold out, and every radio and television station broadcasts the game live. The atmosphere resembles a combination of Thanksgiving and the Superbowl. Victory for the West Indies team is an immediate occasion for national celebration.

Jamaican cricketers are renowned for their bowling and batting, and their fast bowling has particularly caught the imagination of cricket enthusiasts the world over.

In addition to speed, the bowler's skill is measured by his ability to vary his technique so that the batsman is continually surprised. A "googly," for instance, is a ball spun in a counterclockwise motion so that it spins away from the batsman after it bounces, which makes it more difficult to hit. The "off-cutter," on the other hand, spins toward the batsman and if the batsman is not prepared for it, there is a danger that he will miss the ball and have his wicket broken.

THE GAME OF CRICKET

Cricket is played in a stadium with a central 22-yard long rectangular pitch that has a wicket stuck in the ground at either end. (A wicket is a wooden frame made of three vertical $2^1/_2$ feet stumps on top of which are placed two horizontal bails.) Two teams of eleven players a side take turns at bat. The object of the batting side is to score runs. The object of the bowling side is to "dismiss" the batsmen, which can be done in many ways, some of which will be explained below. The game is divided into "innings;" each one ends when 10 batsmen have been dismissed.

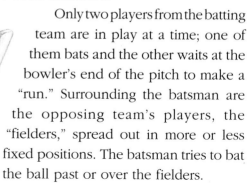

Only two players from the batting team are in play at a time; one of them bats and the other waits at the bowler's end of the pitch to make a "run." Surrounding the batsman are the opposing team's players, the "fielders," spread out in more or less fixed positions. The batsman tries to bat the ball past or over the fielders.

He tries to hit the ball as far as possible, so that while the opposing team is retrieving it, he and his team player can score "runs" by running the 22 yards from one wicket to the other and back again. The opposing team will try to get him "out" by breaking the wicket while they are in mid-run. This is called being "run out." The batsman and his fellow team player will run the pitch

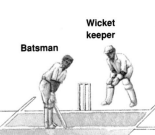

with the intention of exchanging places as many times as possible, because this ensures a higher score.

Keeping score requires a lot of concentration since there are many ways to score. For example, if the ball can be hit high enough to reach the boundary of the playing area without touching the ground, the batsman automatically scores six runs, but if it reaches the boundary area along the ground, then four runs are scored.

The batsman also has the task of defending his wicket with his cricket bat while the bowler attempts to throw the ball past the bat to hit the wicket. If the bowler is successful,

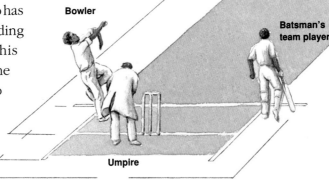

the batsman is "bowled out" and another player on his team takes over. If the bowler is not successful, the batsman meets the ball with his bat and sends it spinning in any direction. The other players on the bowler's team try to catch the ball before it touches the ground, in which case the batsman is out.

Every batsman aspires to reach one hundred runs or a "century," and every batsman's nightmare is to be bowled out without scoring a single run; this is known as being "bowled for a duck."

FESTIVALS

CHRISTMAS IS THE MAJOR RELIGIOUS HOLIDAY in Jamaica, but other Christian festivals such as Ash Wednesday, Good Friday, and Easter Sunday are also public holidays in Jamaica.

INDEPENDENCE DAY AND "FESTIVAL!"

The major festival that brings all Jamaicans together in a celebratory spirit is Independence Day. Although the first Monday in August is the day scheduled for the major events, that day is the culmination of various events and activities in the weeks leading up to it. Throughout July and August, there is a multiplicity of musical, artistic, and dramatic events and parades that come under the banner of "Festival!"

Preparations for the festival begin early in the year. Young people are encouraged to participate through their schools, as each school is involved in the festival in one way or another. Tourists tend to see only the glamorous and colorful displays, but for the students involved, it is an opportunity to learn about their cultural heritage.

MISS JAMAICA

Jamaican women are renowned for their beauty, and each year two beauty contests are held.

In May a Miss Jamaica Universe is chosen, and in September a Miss Jamaica World is crowned. It is the September contest that generates the most excitement because the winner goes on to represent the country in the international Miss World competition. The winner of the Miss World competition is guaranteed fame and fortune, and since 1963, three Jamaican women have won this coveted title, an extraordinary achievement for Jamaica considering its relatively small population.

Opposite: **A procession of "Big Heads" of prominent people is part of the Independence Day celebrations. Here, the head representing former Prime Minister Michael Manley leads the parade.**

The Miss Jamaica World competition begins in earnest in August, for this is when the shortlist of 20 finalists is announced. For weeks afterward, the 20 women are exposed to relentless media attention before appearing at the National Arena in Kingston for the finals.

Despite opposition from those who consider beauty contests to be sexist and insulting to women, the local Miss Jamaica World contests continue to attract a large number of entrants. In previous years, the contest was incorporated into the "Festival!" events. But this came to an end in the 1970s when the government withdrew its support because some social commentators pointed out that finalists in the competition were invariably those with fairer skin color. Since then, the Miss Jamaica World contest has been funded by private organizations.

CHRISTMAS

In Jamaica, the Christmas spirit begins as early as mid-November when, by tradition, grandmothers take out cans of dried fruit and soak it in strong white rum. In December, the dried fruit is poured into cake batter, brown sugar and molasses are added, and the cakes are baked and stored.

Another traditional practice at Christmas involves the making and drinking of sorrel. This is a garnet-colored sweet wine with a spicy flavor that comes from ginger and pimento seeds. Both sorrel and cakes may be stored away and left to "mature," sometimes for many years, but the cakes must be periodically seasoned with liquor.

Unlike in the United States, the exchanging of presents and cards during Christmas is not a custom in Jamaica. One of the main reasons is that the average Jamaican cannot afford it. Another reason is that the majority of Jamaicans still regard the festival as primarily a religious occasion.

Older Jamaicans still remember the days when whole families set out on Christmas Eve for the long walk to a market town to sell their farm produce at the Grand Market. Women bought tins of "wet sugar." Flavored with ginger and nutmeg and left to harden in banana leaves, this became "sugar head," a Christmas treat for children. Special chocolates prepared from dried cocoa pods were also bought. They were then grated into hot milk and sweetened to make a drink known as "chocolate tea."

Above: **Feasting and merrymaking are all part of Christmas.**

Opposite: **A Jamaican, Cindy Breakspeane, was crowned Miss World in 1976.**

107

SPECIAL DAYS IN JAMAICA

Labor Day

Samuel Sharpe (above), who instigated a rebellion of slaves in 1831 and thus started the movement toward the abolition of slavery in 1838, is remembered on this day. He was hanged in the Montego Bay square that is now named after him; an estimated 500 of his fellow rebels were also executed.

National Heroes Day

The third Monday in October draws attention to the country's seven National Heroes. The first of these and the only woman is Nanny of the Maroons. She led her people in guerrilla warfare against colonialists during the first Maroon War between 1720 and 1739. It was said that she could catch the enemy's musket balls and fire them back. Samuel Sharp, who is also commemorated on Labor Day, is another hero for his struggle against slavery. George William Gordon, too, is remembered for fighting against slavery. Gordon, whose mother was a slave and whose father was a planter, championed a movement in the mid-1880s that sought political rights for freed slaves. The fourth hero is Paul Bogle, who campaigned against injustice and poverty and participated in the slave rebellion of 1865 that led to his execution.

The remaining national heroes lived in the 20th century. Marcus Garvey and Alexander Bustamante represented and campaigned for the rights of working class Jamaicans, while Norman Manley is honored for being the founder of the People's National Party and the leader who negotiated Jamaica's independence from Britain.

Independence Day

This day commemorates the events of 1962 when Jamaica became an independent state and the country's new Constitution came into force. The new nation came into existence on August 6, and on the following day, the new Parliament held its first session.

Reggae Sunsplash

First organized in 1978, this week-long celebration of Jamaican music attracts international musicians as well as local groups struggling for success and elusive stardom. One of the most successful Reggae Sunsplash festivals was held in 1981 when Stevie Wonder arrived from the United States to pay tribute to the recently deceased Bob Marley. Montego Bay is the location of this exciting festival, and crowds of more than 150,000 turn up each year. Bands may perform on stage or on the beach (below). The festival begins late each evening and continues into the early hours of the morning, when the more prestigious bands appear.

THE PANTOMIME

A pantomime is an English drama targeted at children, usually produced around Christmas time and based on a fairytale. Jamaican pantomime, on the other hand, is an annual festival held in Kingston that attracts adults and young people alike and has no special association with English fairytales.

The Jamaican pantomime is also performed around Christmas time. And like the English pantomime, Jamaican pantomime has set characters like the Dame (who is always a male actor), a hero, and a heroine. The similarity ends there. In Jamaican pantomime, other characters like Anansi the spider man, have been added. The rhythms of the English music-hall and folk songs have evolved into the drum beats of Pocomania and the movements of the John Canoe dances, and traditional English fairytales have been replaced with stories like "The Pirate Princess," based on the real life events of two female pirates who sailed with Calico Jack in the 17th century.

Another unique feature of the pantomime festival are the short dramatic satires that ridicule government policies and the politicians associated with them. Members of the audience are expected to participate in the performance by throwing in their own humorous contributions.

THE TRADITION OF JOHN CANOE

This tradition dates back to the 17th century when John Canoe and his band of strolling players pranced through the streets for money and food. In the weeks leading up to the Grand Market Day on Christmas Eve, the dancers practice late into the night, trying to coordinate the precise mixing of drum music and dance. The performance is a combination of African dance and European masquerade. Dancers accept small donations of money from spectators to help cover costs, but they are not professionals and their object is not to make a profit.

The dancers are dressed in elaborate animal costumes. The one who takes the part of John Canoe himself is decked

out in a costume that includes symbolic head gear incorporating the tusks of a boar. He always carries a sword, trails the tail of a cow, and leads the procession by a display of his acrobatic skills. His players follow, dressed up to resemble characters from an elite European court, including a king and a queen. Over the years, the procession has become an occasion for performing players to dress up in the spirit of a carnival that has little historical connection with the origin of the processional dance. For instance, a mock police officer will accompany the group pretending to keep them in order, an actor dressed as an extremely pregnant woman will dance along merrily, and a few dancers dressed up as Arawak Indians will join in for good measure.

The John Canoe tradition, or Jonkonnu as it is sometimes called, is associated with Christmas because in the 17th century it was the only time of the year that the slaves had a holiday. The word "Jonkonnu," translated as "sorcerer of death," may be derived from secret societies that existed in West Africa. This may explain the rule that dancers and musicians must communicate with each other by whispering during the procession.

FOOD

ALTHOUGH SUPERMARKETS IN KINGSTON display many of the consumer edibles familiar to North American families, the typical Jamaican diet is based on locally grown foods such as yams, sweet potatoes, breadfruit, bananas, coconuts, and pineapples.

The typical Jamaican kitchen, especially in rural areas, does not depend on electricity but on fuels such as gas, paraffin, or wood. Open-back trucks loaded with gas cylinders are a common sight in towns and villages. Paraffin stoves are also common, and wooden fires are used both indoors and out. Barbecuing outdoors is a way of saving on the cost of fuel. In the larger towns, electricity is more popular among families who can afford to invest in an electric stove.

Above: **Jamaica's congenial weather provides a variety of tropical fruits and vegetables throughout the year.**

Opposite: **Cooking rice and peas in a typical rural kitchen.**

Minimal basic utensils are found in most Jamaican kitchens. The average home is able to do all its cooking with two pots or kerosene tins adapted for this purpose. The large and durable leaves of the banana plant may be used for plates, a custom that Indian laborers were familiar with when they first came to the island.

FOOD HERITAGE

Jamaican food has a distinctive genealogy. It has evolved as a mixture of African, European, Chinese, and Indian cuisines. The slaves brought with them their traditional style of cooking and methods of curing and preserving food. The laborers who came later from China and India brought their respective styles of cooking—light stir-frying and, for curries, slow-cooking. Curried goat, a standard dish at celebrations, is one

113

Ripe ackees, a famous Jamaican fruit.

example of the Indian influence. Rice, Asian spices, and vegetables also came from the Orient via these laborers.

Long before the Europeans arrived in Jamaica, the Arawaks cultivated sweet potatoes, pineapples, and coconuts. Jamaican cuisine still relies on these ingredients. Coconuts, for instance, are readily available and inexpensive and are used in a variety of ways: to make a basic sauce, in cold puddings, and in fudge. The pimento tree is also native to Jamaica where it grows wild on the limestone hills. Its berries, once dried, yield a spice that combines the flavors of clove, nutmeg, and cinnamon. It has earned the name "allspice" and is used in many dishes. Jamaica is the world's largest supplier of pimento.

The ackee tree, on the other hand, was introduced into Jamaica from West Africa towards the end of the 18th century. Its leathery leaves, over 20 feet in height, are a bright orange-red. The three-inch long fruit is poisonous. Inside the fruit are black seeds that contain a fleshy yellow lump, and this is the only edible part.

FAVORITE DISHES

At Sunday lunch, a special family event, the main dish is usually roast beef or chicken. While roast beef betrays an English influence, it tends to be served with rice rather than potatoes. Rice owes its place on the Jamaican table to the Chinese influence. Typical vegetables that accompany a cooked meal include yams, sweet potatoes, pumpkin, and peas.

A very popular dish is a vegetarian stew consisting of rice, peas, red beans, and coconut milk.

Jerked chicken and pork. All Jamaican "jerked" meat has a smoky taste.

Its special taste is enhanced by the use of onions and pepper. Pig's tail or salted beef may be added.

"Ackee and sal'fish" is the national dish. *Sal'fish* refers to the salted fish, which is always served with this dish. It has been eaten at home for as long as Jamaicans can remember, but it only recently began to appear on tourist menus as "authentic Jamaican cuisine." The kidney-shaped yellow flesh removed from the center of the ackee seed has a nutty flavor when cooked. "Ackee and sal'fish" is a small dish, but when a more substantial meal is required, it is served with boiled green bananas, fried plantain and johnny cakes (lightly fried flour dumplings).

"Ackee and sal'fish" is only one example of the numerous seafood dishes eaten by Jamaicans. Others include peppered shrimp, stuffed crayfish, and red snapper. All are accompanied with rice and slices of

Breadfruit is a staple food in Jamaica. The breadfruit tree grows very tall but some of the branches hang low enough for a child to reach and pick the fruit.

onion, peppers, and tomatoes. Some small roadside cafés specialize in serving seafood seasoned with pepper and then roasted on sheets of zinc over an open wood fire.

Another popular roadside dish is "jerked pork," spiced and cooked on an open fire. This was once a Maroon speciality cooked over a fire of green pimento wood. This style of cooking has now spread to other meats like chicken. The food stalls of "jerkers" are a common sight.

An advantage of the country's climate is that fresh fruits are available throughout the year, and the locally-grown fruits provide a rich variety of desserts. Papayas or paw-paws, naseberries, pineapples, or bananas in coconut sauce make a typical end to a family meal.

FOOD GLOSSARY

The names of some Jamaican foods are not commonly found in North America or Europe. Some of the more interesting ones are listed below:

Naseberries
These are small brown fruits with a very soft flesh. They are also called sapodilla.

Stamp-and-go
The local name for quickly fried, bite-sized salted fish. They are often available at roadside food stalls.

Matrimony
Segments of orange covered with mashed star apple, eaten as a dessert, sometimes with cream.

Ortanique (right)
Many species of citrus fruit are used to produce artificial hybrids with exotic names. Ortanique is a hybrid of orange and tangerine. The "ique" in the name was added because the fruit is un*ique*.

Rundown
A meal in itself, consisting of cod or mackerel boiled in coconut milk and then mixed with onions and pepper.

Breadfruit
A large, green fruit about eight inches in diameter that can be roasted, fried, or boiled. It features regularly in the diet because of its 30–40% carbohydrate content. Breadfruit was brought to the island by Captain Bligh in 1793. His earlier attempt to do so caused the famous mutiny by his crew, as depicted in the movie *Mutiny on the Bounty*. The crew rebelled because the captain denied them drinking water, saving it for the breadfruit seedlings. The crew set the captain adrift in a small boat and threw the breadfruit overboard.

RECIPE FOR CURRIED GOAT

(serves 6)
2 large onions
5 lbs young goat meat, cut into cubes
oil or vegetable shortening
2 tablespoons curry powder
1 red pepper
bay leaf
$\frac{1}{2}$ teaspoon allspice
salt and pepper
5–10 fl oz. beef or chicken stock
8 fl oz. coconut milk
a squeeze of lime juice

Sauté onions and brown meat in oil/shortening. Add curry powder and red pepper. Stir over medium heat for three minutes. Add bay leaf, allspice, salt, pepper, and stock. Simmer for at least two hours. Add coconut milk and simmer for another 30 minutes. Add lime juice just before serving.

RECIPE FOR PLANTAIN FRITTERS

$4\frac{1}{2}$ tablespoons self-raising flour
6 tablespoons plain flour
$\frac{1}{2}$ cup water
$\frac{3}{4}$ teaspoon sugar
2 plantains, each peeled and sliced into 4 pieces
sufficient oil for deep-frying
a squeeze of lime juice

Sift both kinds of flour into a bowl. Pour in water and stir till a smooth paste is obtained. Batter should be thick enough to coat plantain. If it is too thin, add more plain flour. Add sugar and stir well.

Heat oil in a deep pan until it is smoking hot. Coat each plantain section with batter and slide into oil. Fry for 5 minutes till golden brown. Serve with a squeeze of lime juice.

DRINKS

Popular Jamaican drinks are made using coconut water and goat's milk. The abundance of fruit provides opportunities for many delicious flavors to be blended by mixing different juices. One popular beverage is made by mixing tamarind juice, soursop (a fruit), and coconut water.

Coffee is the most common beverage. One type of coffee that is grown in Jamaica is reputed to have such an exceptional taste that it commands the highest price of any brand of coffee in the world. It is named after the Blue Mountains where the berries of the Blue Mountain Yacca produce red coffee berries. Coffee was first brewed by the Arabs of Yemen from the

seeds of a small evergreen tree *Coffea arabica*. It was introduced to Jamaica in 1728.

Alcohol plays a significant role in Jamaican culture. Bars are found everywhere and provide a central focus for socializing. No one type of drink is especially popular, although cold beer is ubiquitous. A local brand called Red Stripe has the nickname "The Policeman" because the Jamaican police uniform has a red stripe on the pants. More expensive drinks are the various liqueurs, some of which, like Tia Maria, have become standard items in bars and liquor stores around the world.

Jamaica's most famous drink is rum. Rum is often blended with different fruits to produce unique fruit liquors. It is also widely used in fruit punches, the most popular being planter's punch, a blend of lime juice, syrup, and rum, flavored with angostura bitters and cooled with plenty of crushed ice.

Jamaican bars are famous for their imaginative drinks. Typical equipment used for mixing cocktails includes shakers and implements for measuring, stirring, and straining.

Inside a rum distillery.

THE STORY OF RUM

Rum is a spirit distilled from freshly crushed sugarcane or from the fermentation of molasses, a by-product of the sugarcane industry.

Slaves were encouraged to make rum, and the drink was readily available to everyone working on sugar plantations. It was used to help pacify the laborers and deal with the discontent and unhappiness caused by their forced removal from their homeland.

When Jamaica was wrested from the Spanish by the English, rum was introduced to England for the first time. It received a major boost in its popularity when the British navy decided, for the same motives as the plantation owners, to dispense a free amount of the drink to all sailors.

Rum is distilled wherever sugarcane is grown, but Jamaican rum is the most famous of all. What gives rum its unique quality is that sugar is present from the very beginning of the distilling process. Other spirits such as whisky and gin depend on an initial stage of malting when starch is converted to sugar. Because the distillation of rum does not require this stage, it is purer and the original flavor is retained.

JAMAICAN RUM

What gives rum from Jamaica a special status lies in the special process of distilling. Each distillery has its own unique process of adding flavors and blending, and this makes one brand of rum different from another. The most famous brand in Jamaica is Appleton rum, made by Wray and Nephew in Kingston, although its sugar estates are in the southwest of the country.

Rums of different ages, depending on how many years they have been left to mature in wooden casks, are blended together to

produce the special Appleton taste. The wooden casks must be kept as cool as possible so as to minimize loss through evaporation. The warehouses have special roofs that allow water to run over them constantly and keep the temperature down to an acceptable level. A distillery like that of Wray and Nephew keeps the details of its actual blending process a secret so as to maintain the exclusivity of its brand.

Prestigious Jamaican rums may be stored for up to 15 years before they are available for sale and export. Appleton Special rum is sold in over 800 cities around the world. When President Reagan visited Jamaica, he was presented with a case of Appleton rum that was over 100 years old.

Jamaicans drink many different types of rum. For many people, their favorite rum will be one distilled according to a traditional recipe and made only for local consumption. It is most likely to be a white rum and in a very pure form—100 proof (the measure of the purity of alcohol).

The international brands have been adulterated so that their proof is reduced. Adulterating rum adds to the cost of the final drink, which is another reason why pure white rum is inexpensive and more popular. Practitioners of traditional medicine use the cheap white rum as a rubbing lotion for backache. Ganja soaked in white rum and smoked is highly regarded as a general cure-all for minor medical complaints.

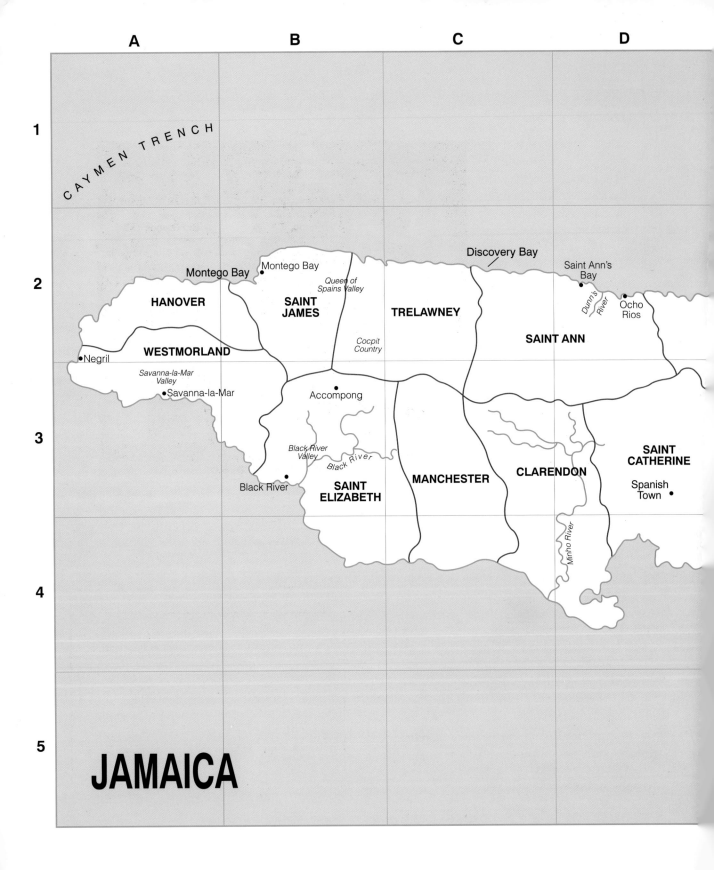

JAMAICA

E F

Annotto Bay

SAINT MARY

PORTLAND

Rio Grande

Port Antonio

THE BLUE MOUNTAINS

Hector's River

SAINT ANDREW

Yallahs River

Kingston

Blue Mountain Peak

SAINT THOMAS

Port Royal

Morant Bay

Morant Bay

Kingston Harbour

CARIBBEAN SEA

N

Accompong	B3	Negril	A2
Annotto Bay	E3		
		Ocho Rios	D2
Black River	B3		
Black River Valley	B3	Port Antonio	F3
Blue Mountains	E3	Portland	E3
Blue.Mountain Peak	E3	Port Royal	E4
Caribbean Sea	E4	Queen of Spains Valley	B2
Caymen Trench	A1		
Clarendon	C3	Rio Grande	F3
Cockpit Country	B2		
		Saint Ann's Bay	D2
Discovery Bay	C2	Saint Catherine	D3
Dunn's River	D2	Saint Elizabeth	B3
		Saint James	B2
Hanover	A2	Saint Mary	E3
Hector's River	F3	Saint Thomas	F3
		Savanna-la Mar	A3
Kingston	E3	Savanna-la-Mar Valley	A3
Kingston Harbor	E3	Spanish Town	D3
		Trelawney	C2
Manchester	C3		
Minho River	D3, D4	Westmorland	A2
Montego Bay	B2		
Morant Bay	F4	Yallahs River	E3

— Parish Boundary

▲ Mountain

● Capital

● City

River

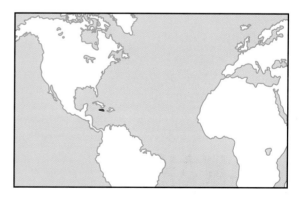

QUICK NOTES

LAND AREA
4,244 square miles
146 miles (east-west)
50 miles (north-south)

POPULATION
2.4 million (1990)

CAPITAL
Kingston

NATIONAL FLOWER
Lignum vitae, "wood of life," purple with
bright yellow stamens

NATIONAL BIRD
Streamer-tailed hummingbird

OFFICIAL LANGUAGE
English

MAJOR RELIGION
Christianity

HIGHEST POINT
Blue Mountain Peak (7,400 feet)

NATIONAL FLAG
A gold diagonal cross with black triangular
side panels, and green triangular panels at
top and bottom.

REGIONS
Clarendon, Hanover, Manchester, Portland,
St. Andrew (and Kingston), St. Ann, St.
Catherine, St. Elizabeth, St. James, St. Mary,
St. Thomas, Trelawney, and Westmorland.

MAIN EXPORTS
Agricultural—sugarcane, bananas, cacao,
coffee
Industrial—alumina, bauxite, tourism

IMPORTANT ANNIVERSARIES
Independence Day, the first Monday in
August
National Heroes Day, the third Monday in
October

LEADERS IN POLITICS
Alexander Bustamante—prime minister
1962–1967
Norman Manley—founder of the People's
National Party in 1938
Edward Seaga—prime minister 1980–1989
Michael Manley—prime minister 1972–1980
and 1989–1992

LEADERS IN THE ARTS
Louise Bennett (poet and folklorist)
Victor Reid, Roger Mais (novelists)
Edna Manley (sculptress)
Bob Marley, Jimmy Cliff (reggae musicians)

GLOSSARY

ackee	Type of fruit. Only the flesh inside the seeds of this fruit can be eaten.
buccaneers	Pirates or sea robbers.
duppy	Ghosts or spirits.
ganja	("GAN-jah") Marijuana, a plant that has narcotic effects when smoked.
kimbanda	("kim-BAHN-dah") A large drum usually covered with goatskin. It produces a bass sound.
kumina	("KOO-mi-nah") A cult of animism.
Maroons	A term originally used to refer to the freed and fugitive African slaves living in the mountains. Now, the term refers to their descendants who continue to live in their villages in a more inaccessible part of central Jamaica.
mento	Music and dance descended from the slaves from Africa. The most prominent feature of mento is the regular beat of drums.
mulattoes	Progeny of European and African unions.
obeah	("OH-be-uh") A form of witchcraft.
ortanique	Juicy fruit obtained by crossing an orange and a tangerine.
patois	Dialect differing generally from the accepted standard of the language.
plain kyas	A drum similiar to the *kimbanda* but much smaller in size. It produces a treble sound.
plantain	A type of banana that requires cooking before it can be eaten.
Pocomania	A hybrid faith, the result of the combination of animistic and Christian beliefs.
tam	Woollen knitted cap worn by males, especially Rastafarians.
zombie	Spirits of deceased family members or friends that are invoked in animism rituals.

BIBLIOGRAPHY

Abrahams, P.: *Jamaica—An Island Mosaic*, Her Majesty's Stationery Office, London, 1957.

Booth, E.: *Jamaica and the Greater Antilles*, The Crowood Press, Swindon, UK, 1991.

Cargill, M. (Ed): *Ian Fleming Introduces Jamaica*, Andre Deutsch, London, 1965.

Cassidy and Page: *Dictionary of Jamaican English*, Cambridge University Press, 1980.

Floyd, Barry: *Jamaica—An Island Microcosm*, St Martin's Press, New York, 1979.

Insight Guides: *Jamaica*, APA Publications, Hongkong, 1991.

Sherlock, Philip: *Keeping Company with Jamaica*, Macmillan Caribbean, 1984.

Springer, E. P.: *The Caribbean, the Lands and Their People*, Macdonald Educational, London, 1987.

INDEX

INDEX

INDEX